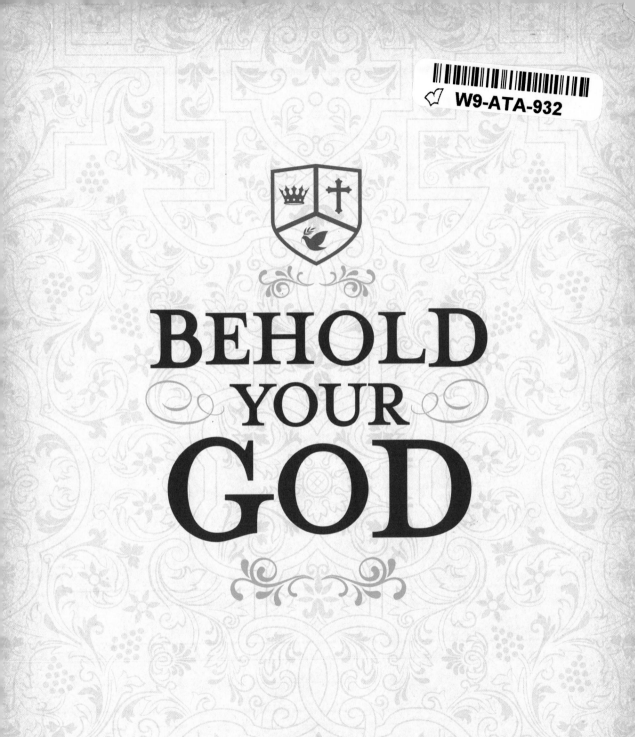

BEHOLD YOUR GOD

W9-ATA-932

PositiveAction
BIBLE CURRICULUM

BEHOLD YOUR GOD

Copyright © 1980, 2000, 2010, 2016 by Positive Action for Christ, Inc., P.O. Box 700, 502 W. Pippen St., Whitakers, NC 27891.

All rights reserved. No part may be reproduced in any manner without permission in writing from the publisher.

First edition published 1980

Fourth edition published 2016
Second printing, 2017

Printed in the United States of America

ISBN: 978-1-59557-203-5

First edition by Frank Hamrick and Jeff Hedgepeth
Revised and expanded by Jim Lord
Managing Editor: C.J. Harris, Ph.D.
Designer: Shannon Brown
Artwork by Chris Ellison

Published by

Table of Contents

Preface

As the Source of all truth, God is in fact the highest truth we can study. Our view of Him affects every other belief and practice. Therefore, we wrote this curriculum to inspire you to explore the heights and depths of His majesty—because while God lies above and beyond our understanding, He has also chosen to make Himself known to us.

In Hebrews 11:6, we read that we must accept two things by faith:

- That God exists
- That He rewards those who seek Him

From this starting point, we can begin to study the incomparable God described in Scripture. Like a little child walking alongside her father, we may not understand the height of God's holiness or the fullness of His grace, but we can feel the strength of His hand holding ours.

As Christ prayed for all His followers in John 17:20–26, we pray that you would know God, trust in His love, and be unified together in Him.

In This Study

Student Work

Each chapter in this study includes some reading and exercises that you will likely complete by yourself outside of class. As you read and analyze passages from Scripture, you will record your findings and thoughts in the blanks provided. These exercises should increase your understanding of the material covered by your teacher. As you complete this work, be sure to note any questions you might have for your teacher—or any topics you might like to study further.

Notes from the Teacher's Lesson

Included also is a brief outline that your teacher should cover in class. As you listen to your teacher, fill in the blanks provided, and look up the Scripture references in your Bible.

Application Activities

Your teacher may assign some of the extra activities listed at the end of each chapter. These include reading assignments and short writing projects that will encourage you to examine your beliefs in light of Scripture.

Testing and Evaluation

Your teacher will explain testing policies and expectations for your class. Quiz and test questions may relate to your student exercises, the teacher's lesson, or both. Your teacher may also ask you to memorize passages of Scripture that relate to each lesson.

UNIT 1
The Knowledge of God

"It is not what a man does that determines whether his work is sacred or secular; it is why he does it. The motive is everything."

—A. W. Tozer, *The Pursuit of God*

PHIL. 3:10-11

ISA 43:7

COL. 1:16

1 PT 3:5

PS 19:1

ΙΧΘΥΣ

CHAPTER 1

Laying the Foundation

"Glorifying God has respect to all the persons of the Trinity; it respects God the Father, who gave us life; God the Son, who lost His life for us; and God the Holy Ghost, who produces a new life in us."

—Thomas Watson, *A Body of Divinity*

Thomas Carlyle, a Scottish historian and philosopher in the nineteenth century, wrote,

> "The man without a purpose is like a ship without a rudder—a waif, a nothing, a no man. Have a purpose in life, and, having it, throw such strength of mind and muscle into your work as God has given you."

This advice is especially important for Christian teenagers. You stand at the edge of adulthood, with growing liberties and growing responsibilities. You've begun to realize that life extends beyond your day-to-day experiences—that what you do now will impact your life weeks, months, and even years in the future. So many activities and amusements and causes clamor for your attention, and perhaps you've begun to ask yourself, "How do I choose from all this? What purpose guides my choice?"

God has a purpose and plan for each of His children, and we're responsible to discover that purpose—and pursue it. Our focus and goal will then guide how we work, how we serve others, how we rest, and how we grow.

The teacher's lesson for this chapter establishes the highest purpose for every Christian—namely, to glorify God. In everything we do, we should reflect God's character.

To do this, however, we depend on His Spirit to mold us into a better image of Him. We depend on His Word to help us know Him, personally and intimately. It's not enough to know *about* God—we must know God *Himself.*

Keep this goal in mind as you proceed through this study. Seek God, not simply knowledge about Him. Know His work in your life. Discover the truth He's placed in His Word for you. Ask Him to reveal Himself to you, and ask Him to help you reflect His love and truth.

. . . .

Student Work

We Can Seek God Only Through Faith

Why is faith necessary to seek God? While the Bible points to a great deal of *evidence* that God exists, it does not try to *prove* that He does. From the very first verse, Scripture simply assumes His presence. Genesis 1:1 states that in the beginning, God created the heavens and the Earth—no introduction necessary. From the rest of Scripture, we learn more about who God is and what He does, but nowhere in these words does God lay out a systematic proof of His existence.

Further, we can find no definitive proof for God in either science or philosophy. As much as we can see order in the universe, as much as we can feel that we were created for some higher, spiritual purpose, as much as we know in our heart of hearts that life means something more—these signs all point to God, but they do not prove beyond all possible doubt that He is there. Many people see this evidence, yet never believe in God.

But why can't we write a step-by-step proof that God exists?

Only God Can Prove Himself

We are not the judges of God. Even if we could somehow establish beyond all doubt that God exists, that still wouldn't be enough to sustain our belief. How could we possibly prove that this God is the God that the Bible describes?

To explore this idea, let's look at a few passages that describe God's power.

God Is Omnipotent

| *omni* / all | + | *potent* / powerful |

✎ Read Exodus 6:2–3. By what name did God appear to Abraham, Isaac, and Jacob? _He said, that "he is the lord"_

This is one of God's most important names—rendered in Hebrew as *El Shaddai*. God is the all-powerful Creator of the universe (Jer. 32:17). With Him, all things are possible. He can do whatever He wants to do (Ps. 115:3).

God Is Omniscient

| *omni* / all | + | *science* / knowledge |

✎ Read 1 John 3:20. What does this verse say that God knows?

_____

✎ According to Psalm 147:5, is there any limit to His understanding?

_____

Nothing is hidden from God's sight (Heb. 4:13).

God Is Eternal and Immutable

| *eternal* / enduring / everlasting / without beginning or end |

| *immutable* / unchanging |

Further, we read in Psalm 102:12 that God endures across eternity. He is the same yesterday, today, and forever (Heb. 13:8). He has always been, and He will always be (Rev. 4:8). He calls Himself the forever "I AM" (Exo. 3:14; John 8:58).

How could we prove that a Being is all-powerful, all-knowing, and transcendent above time itself?

- Would we force God to *do* everything He could possibly do? Would we be like Gideon in Judges 6:36–40, asking God to prove His power by keeping a fleece wet or dry?

- Or would we ask Him to recite all knowledge—to give us the position and properties of every bit of matter and energy in the universe?

- Would we ask Him to justify His every thought and action in terms we could understand?

- Would we then travel across all time—and whatever lies above and beyond time—to prove that God has never changed, nor ever will?

How could we even begin to absorb all of the information required to pass judgment on such a Being? A person would have to stand *above* God to witness the scope of His power—and no such person could exist. As we read in Job 39 and 40, no one can ever begin to comprehend even a fraction of God's power.

And the attributes mentioned above speak only to God's ability. We haven't even touched on His holiness, His love, the rest of His character, or the scope of His work in our hearts. How could we prove that He is loving, just, and true?

Only God can answer that question—we can't depend on our own wisdom. While we can find many things in this world that tell us that our belief in God is good and reasonable, and while we can admire how God has preserved the truth and consistency of His Word, the Bible, we shouldn't expect to find proof that negates our need for faith.

✎ Read the summary of Enoch's life in Hebrews 11:5–6. According to verse 6, what two things can a person believe only through faith?

_____

_____

_____

_____

God Asks Us to Trust Him

God chose to provide us with His goodness and grace through *faith*—that is, our trust in Him.

✎ Read Hebrews 11:1. What is faith? _now_
faith is confidence in what
we do not see.

_____

_____

✎ According to verse 3, what is one of the first things we accept by faith?

— faith that Jesus died and rose again and saved us
— I believe that God never changes
— I believe that there is purpose for each person.

God asks us to believe Him when He says that the physical universe—the things that we can see and touch and detect—originally came from Him. No matter how far back scientists and philosophers try to peer into our past, they will always reach a point of uncertainty, a place where geology and mathematics and physics break down, where they can only guess and speculate as to what came before. When we reach that point, and when we wonder what or Who began all this, Scripture asks us to accept God as the answer.

Science and philosophy can only bring us so close to God. He's chosen faith as the invisible bridge to lead us the rest of the way.

Is this a blind faith? Does the Creator of our minds and our eyes expect us to ignore logic and evidence? Certainly not.

God Gave Us His Creation

✎ According to Colossians 1:16, why did God make all things?

✎ So what then does Psalm 19:1–6 say the heavens show us?

✎ And according to Romans 1:19–20, where can we find another glimpse of God's character or attributes?

All of nature exists as a celebration of God's majesty. While the world has fallen under the curse of sin, and it is no longer a perfect reflection of its Creator, we can still see a glimpse of God's power and character in the visible universe.

God Gave Us His Word

In the Bible, we find 66 books written by men and women across three continents over roughly 1,500 years. But in this veritable library of Scripture, we can find a consistency and a cohesion explained only by the inspiration of God (1 Tim. 3:16–17; 2 Pet. 1:21).

He guided the experiences and thoughts of these writers to give us a sufficient account of His character and work through history—an account more specific and helpful than the glimpse we see in Creation.

And most importantly, God's Word reveals the cornerstone of our faith— Jesus Christ.

God Gave Us His Son

To be clear—when we say that Jesus is God's Son, we do not mean that Jesus is somehow the biological offspring of God the Father. In the New Testament Greek, the phrase υἱὸς εἶ τοῦ Θεοῦ (*huios ei tou theos*; "the Son of God") is used to describe Jesus as being of the same *nature*, or likeness, as God. He is *from* God, because He *is* God Himself.

If that sounds confusing, it's because it is. But don't worry. We'll explore the doctrine of the Trinity later—specifically, that God exists eternally in three Persons, though also as one united Being.

In Jesus we see God revealed as a Man—as a Person who faced temptation, hunger, and all the hardships we know, and yet still perfectly reflected the love and truth of the Father.

✎ Read John 17:3–4. Here Jesus prayed to the Father on the night before His crucifixion. What do these verses say about Christ's purpose for coming to Earth?

_____

_____

_____

_____

Christ came to Earth to connect us to God—so that we could be free from the bondage of sin, and so we could be holy like Him.

In Jesus we see the abstract doctrines of God made clear and real. We see God's holiness in the way Christ lived without sin, in the way He preached righteousness and called others to do the same.

We see God's love in the way He reached out to sinners, the lost and the forsaken, and how He gave up His life to redeem us.

And we see God's power in the way He healed the sick, fed the hungry, calmed the storms, raised the dead, and indeed conquered Death itself by rising from the grave.

The ancient world did not turn upside down over a myth or legend. Thousands and even millions of people did not risk imprisonment and death to follow a mad itinerant preacher—they responded to the calling and work of God Himself.

God Gave Us His Spirit

When Jesus ascended back into heaven, He did not leave His followers alone.

✎ Read John 14:16–17. What did Jesus promise that God would send after He left? Be specific.

_____

_____

✎ And in Acts 2:1–4, how did God's Spirit first mark His arrival?

_____

_____

_____

_____

God showed everyone in Jerusalem that these believers were His children, gifted with the ability to reach across languages and culture to share the new gospel of Christ.

And today He performs an equally amazing miracle in those who have accepted Christ—He makes us *like* Jesus. He sets us apart (Rom. 15:15–16), strengthening us so that we can better know God's love and share that love with others (Eph. 3:14–19). He grows within us love, joy, peace, patience, kindness, goodness, faithfulness, meekness, and self-control (Gal. 5:22–23). He makes us holy.

If there's one thing we can learn from culture, politics, and indeed all of anthropology (*anthropo* / humanity + *-logy* / learning / study)—it's that people can't change themselves in any meaningful way. We're all destined to fail and disappoint each other if we work in our own power.

But the Spirit guides us to a truer and better purpose. And as we see His work in our lives, we learn to trust God with our minds and with our hearts. We are the blessed ones whom God leads to believe in Christ, even though we have not yet seen Him with our eyes (John 17:20–21; 20:29).

God Will Reveal Himself Fully Later

One day, we will have no need for faith. At the end of all things, God will reveal Himself to all people, establishing once and for all His majesty (Rev. 21:3–4). Every knee will bow to God, and every tongue will confess that He *is* (Rom. 14:11–12).

God has chosen to delay His final revelation until that time, when all will be explained, when all will be answered—and when every tear will be wiped away from our eyes (Rev. 21:4).

Jesus will not arrive on Earth, ready to usher in His eternal kingdom, only to find that we have proved all there is to know about Him. He will not break apart the heavens only to pat us on the back for everything we've discovered. Rather, He will destroy the wickedness gathered against Him (Rev. 19:11, 19–20), and He will build a new Creation, one where God and humanity can finally dwell together (Rev. 21:1–5).

Challenge

God created us to glorify Him. To glorify Him, we must be like Him. To be like Him, we must know Him. To know Him, we must love and trust Him in faith.

Make no mistake—this study can help you learn about God, but you'll need His grace to love Him, trust Him, know Him, reflect Him, and glorify Him. As you read and study His Word, ask God to keep you close to Himself.

This will not be easy. As we read in 2 Peter 3:4–9, people will mock our faith, tempting us to doubt Christ's promise to return, or to forget His rule over Creation.

But God is not slow to fulfill His promise. Time means nothing to Him. He has appointed a day for His judgment, and He waits only because He is patient to receive any who repent and turn to Him. We serve the almighty, eternal God, and His promises are as sure now as they will be when we see them fulfilled.

✎ What is the purpose of our faith? Read Philippians 3:8–11, and write verses 10 and 11 below.

I want to know Christ - yes, to know the Power of his ressuration and Participation in his sufferings, becoming like hime in tae death, and so Somehow, attaining to the ressuration from the dead.

Seek God in faith, and ask Him to glorify Himself in you.

Notes from the Teacher's Lesson

Our Goal

- To Grow Closer and Closer to Christ.

Knowing, Being, and Doing

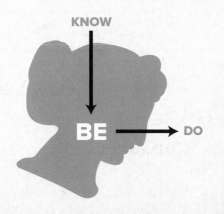

- Knowing:

  Knowing that God will
  never leave me nor
  forsake me.

- Being:

  I need to be Patient with
  People and I need to hold on to his truths

- Doing:

  I need to show others
  love through my actions
  and patience and hold my
  tough when I should not
  say things I should
  not.

- Which is most important? _Praise God_ (Eph. 1:12)

The Doctrine of Holiness

- God _Calls_ us to holiness (1 Pet. 1:14–16).

  ○ God's holiness encompasses two main ideas:

  - God is _light_, without sin (1 John 1:5).
  - God is _High/Holy_ above all (Isa. 57:15).

  ○ Our personal holiness is . . .

  - The work that _Christ_ performs in us
  - To set us apart *from* _sin_ and *to* righteousness
  - So that we reflect God's _holyness_

- Jesus _Calls_ us to holiness (Eph. 5:25–27).
- God's Spirit _transforms_ our holiness (2 Cor. 3:18).

Application Activities

1. Make eight separate lists, labeling each with one of the following headings. Give yourself plenty of room for each list.

   - Health & Fitness
   - Financial & Material
   - Social
   - Family
   - Career & Calling
   - Academic
   - Spiritual
   - Other

   - Under each label, list your hopes, dreams, and goals.

   - Then for each item, ask yourself, "Can I pursue this goal to God's glory?" If not, strike it from your list. But if so, write a brief explanation of how the goal will help you better reflect the love and truth of God.

2. Read Job 38–40. In these passages, God appears to Job, a good man who lost his riches and his family, and who had begun to question God's wisdom.

   - Write a brief summary of God's response to Job, using two paragraphs or less. Note especially Job 38:4–7; 40:2, 8–14; and perhaps Job 42:10–17.

   - If you believe any other passages in the Bible might give us a more complete perspective on God's plan, list them below your summary.

3. In Thomas Watson's *A Body of Divinity*, read or skim the chapter entitled "On Man's Chief End."

   - List from the chapter the four things that Watson argues are part of glorifying God.

   - List also the seventeen ways he suggests that we can glorify God.

   - If you find something in this chapter with which you disagree, write a short counterargument, supported by Scripture, below your list.

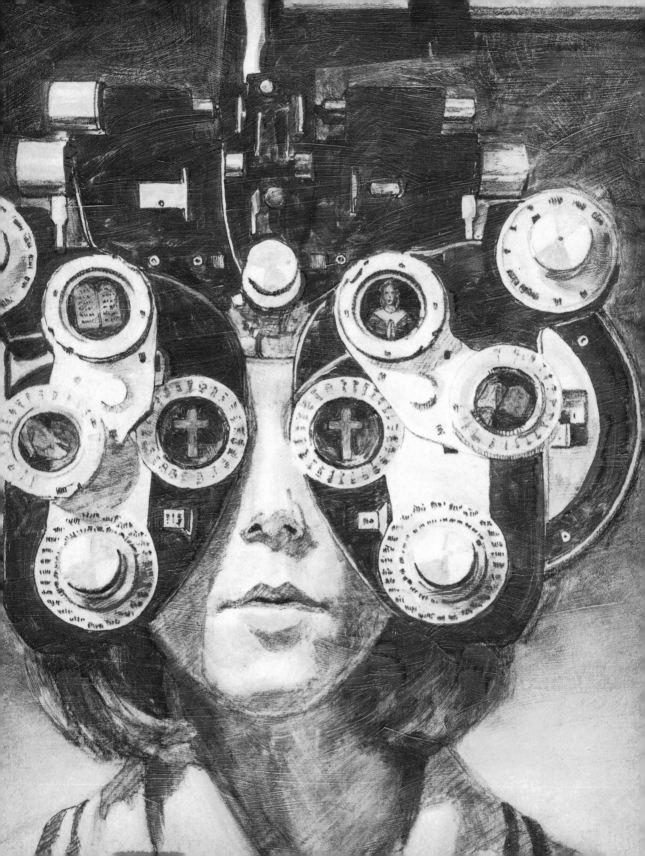

CHAPTER 2

Getting a Right Focus

"God must be the Terminus ad quem, *the ultimate end of all actions."*
—Thomas Watson, *A Body of Divinity*

We are sacred beings, not in the sense that we have some sort of mystical power, but that God created us to reflect some higher, spiritual meaning. When He made Adam and Eve, He gave them both His image (Gen. 1:27)—that is, the capacity to in some way reflect His thoughts. We exist as flesh and blood, but through Christ, our spirit can commune with God (John 4:23–24).

Just like a painting is more than colorful brushstrokes on a canvas, we are more than atoms or cells or organs. We represent the design of a good and creative God, and our thoughts of love and grace can mirror His own, at least in a small way.

This spiritual dimension to our being lets us look at the world in a way that animals could not. We see order and beauty in nature and in art. We resonate with the themes of literature, delving into the meaning of language and exploring concepts that could never be captured by the written word. And when we look at other people, we see men and women blessed with the image of God—people we should respect, love, and cherish.

Likewise, when we look at the Bible, we can focus beyond its immediate value to its eternal purpose. We see more than a body of literature—more than a set of stories and rules. We find in Scripture a glimpse of the God who gave us His Word so that we could better know and love Him.

We honor the commandments in the Bible because we honor our holy God. We learn from the stories because we want to learn from their Author. We rejoice in the gospel of grace because we rejoice in its Architect. We do not merely study heroes and villains, prophets and kings, apostles and teachers, but rather the God who used imperfect men and women to showcase His glory.

Student Work

Our Goal

✎ Read Ephesians 1:3–6. What happened because God chose us? That is, how did He affect us (v. 4)?

_____

_____

✎ And what was the ultimate reason for adopting us into His family (v. 6)?

_____

_____

God sanctified us—that is, He set us apart in holiness—for His own glory, and so that we could share in His grace. Our goal, likewise, should be to magnify His glory.

The Path to Our Goal

Love

Our love for God fuels our desire to be like Him—to *be* holy and then reflect His holiness with our actions.

✎ Read 1 John 4:7–12. According to these verses, how did God show love to us (vv. 9–10)?

_____

_____

✎ What should be our response to God's love for us (v. 11)?

_____

_____

✎ And as we show our love for God by loving other people, what two things does God do for us (v. 12)?

_____

_____

As we love the same way that God loves us, He will work in our hearts.

We see the same principle between a married couple. As they love each other over many years, they can gradually think, act, and sometimes even look alike.

The Word

In the life of David, we find an example of a person who . . .

- Studied the Word
- Saw God in the Word
- Grew to love God
- And therefore sought to be holy like God
- And then serve God

While David was far from perfect, the attitude he demonstrated in Psalm 119 serves as an excellent model for us today.

The Object of His Focus

✎ In Psalm 119:1–3, how does David describe those who are holy, and therefore blessed?

- v. 1—They are blameless and undefiled as they walk in the way. They walk _____.

- v. 2—They keep _____. They seek _____ with all their heart.

- v. 3—They do no _____. But they instead _____.

✎ Whom must we follow to be holy? _____

✎ What do you think it means to seek God?

_____

_____

_____

_____

_____

_____

The Method of His Focus

✎ How did David "see" the Lord? Verses 11, 15, and 16 of Psalm 119 suggest four ways. Read each of those verses, then look at the following methods of study. Write a phrase from the psalm that most closely matches each method.

1. Memorizing the Word:

   _____

   _____

2. Meditating on the Word:

   _____

   _____

3. Enjoying the Word:

   _____

   _____

4. Reviewing verses for memory's sake:

   _____

   _____

We do not love God simply by studying the Word. We study God in His Word so that we love Him even more.

✎ What other—less helpful—reasons might people have to study the Bible?

_____

_____

_____

_____

_____

✎ Can some good come from this kind of study? _____

✎ But did God give us His Word primarily for those reasons? _____

✎ Read verse 18. What does David ask God to help him see?

_____

_____

✎ Some of the later verses in Psalm 119 give us an idea of what these were. Read each verse below, and record what David wanted to see.

- v. 27b – _____

- v. 41 – _____

- v. 52 – _____

The Result of His Focus

✎ As David meditated on what he saw of God, he grew to love God more. In each of the following verses, what part of God's work or character did David see?

- v. 62 – _____
  _____

- v. 68 – _____
  _____

- v. 73 – _____
  _____

- v. 77 – _____
  _____

- v. 88 – _____
  _____

✎ This love in turn drove David to confess the following:

- v. 94 – I am _____

- v. 125 – I am _____

As we focus on God in His Word, He grows our love for Him, which in turn fuels our desire to be like Him. And as He makes us more holy, we serve Him and magnify His glory to others.

We call this process of increasing holiness *sanctification*.

Notes from the Teacher's Lesson

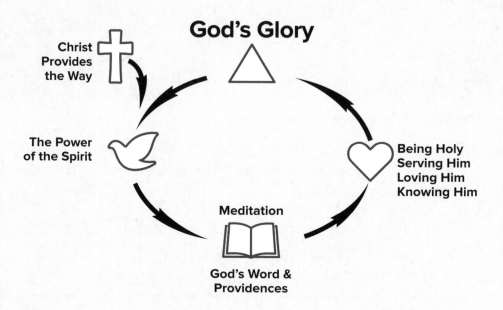

God's Glory

Christ Provides the Way

The Power of the Spirit

Meditation

God's Word & Providences

Being Holy
Serving Him
Loving Him
Knowing Him

The Results of a Wrong Focus

Wrong Focus	Common Result
Holiness	• Dependence on _____ • Neglect of _____
The Word	• _____ | *ortho* / right | + | *dox* / teaching |
Love	• Redefinition of _____ • Neglect of God's _____
Rules and Laws	• _____—dependence on our own works for salvation and holiness

Wrong Focus	Common Result
Doing	• Directionless _____
Being	• Self-improvement without _____

The Right Focus

- On a Person: _____ (Phil. 3:20–21)
- Through the _____ (1 Cor. 13:12)
- Through _____

The Results of the Right Focus

- A love for _____
- Genuine _____

Application Activities

1. Read the first verse of every psalm listed below, and record on a separate sheet everything mentioned about God. Be sure to include the reference next to each truth. Then find at least five more psalms that open with a truth about God, and list those, as well.

    Psalms 7, 8, 9, 18, 19, 23, 25, 27, 30, and 42.

2. Read Philippians 3:4–15, and then answer the following questions about the passage.

    A. In what things did Paul take pride before he accepted Christ?
    B. Where did he focus after he was redeemed (vv. 8, 10)?
    C. Toward what goal did he strive after his salvation (vv. 13–14)?
    D. What do you think Paul meant by what he wrote in verse 15?

3. Jesus Christ sought to do the will of His Father (John 5:30). Based on your knowledge of the life and ministry of Christ, describe briefly how He pursued this mission in each of the following situations. Cite an example from Scripture for each item.

    A. When He was angry
    B. When He ate and fellowshipped with others
    C. When He faced temptation
    D. When He heard about others' misfortune
    E. When He heard about others' blessings
    F. When He prayed

    In what ways can you better follow Christ's example?

CHAPTER 3

Knowing God

"To glorify God is to have God-admiring thoughts, to esteem Him most excellent, and search for diamonds in this rock only."

—Thomas Watson, *A Body of Divinity*

The last chapter challenged you to know God. But you might ask now, "Isn't God too big, too powerful, and too complicated for anyone to know Him?"

And you'd be right. No one could ever fully grasp the enormity of God's character and power. But as A. W. Tozer, a twentieth century preacher and author, wrote in his book *The Pursuit of God*:

> To most people God is an inference, not a reality. He is a deduction . . . but He remains personally unknown to the individual. "He must be," they say, "therefore we believe He is." Others do not go even so far as this; they know of Him only by hearsay. They have never bothered to think the matter out for themselves, but have heard about Him from others, and have put belief in Him into the back of their minds along with the various odds and ends that make up their total creed. To many others God is but an ideal, another name for goodness, or beauty, or truth; or He is law, or life, or the creative impulse back of the phenomena of existence.
>
> These notions about God are many and varied, but they who hold them have one thing in common: they do not know God in personal experience. The possibility of intimate acquaintance with Him has not entered their minds. While admitting His existence they do not think of Him as knowable in the sense that we know things or people.

Christians, to be sure, go further than this, at least in theory. Their creed requires them to believe in the personality of God, and they have been taught to pray, "Our Father, which art in heaven." Now personality and fatherhood carry with them the idea of the possibility of personal acquaintance. This is admitted, I say, in theory, but for millions of Christians, nevertheless, God is no more real than He is to the non-Christian. They go through life trying to love an ideal and be loyal to a mere principle.

Over against all this cloudy vagueness stands the clear scriptural doctrine that God can be known in personal experience. A loving Personality dominates the Bible, walking among the trees of the garden and breathing fragrance over every scene. Always a living Person is present, speaking, pleading, loving, working, and manifesting Himself whenever and wherever His people have the receptivity necessary to receive the manifestation.

The Bible assumes as a self-evident fact that men can know God with at least the same degree of immediacy as they know any other person or thing that comes within the field of their experience. The same terms are used to express the knowledge of God as are used to express knowledge of physical things. "O taste and see that the Lord is good." "All thy garments smell of myrrh, and aloes, and cassia, out of the ivory palaces." "My sheep hear My voice." "Blessed are the pure in heart, for they shall see God." These are but four of countless such passages from the Word of God. And more important than any proof text is the fact that the whole import of the Scripture is toward this belief.

If God did not want us to know Him personally and intimately, why then did He give us the Scriptures? As we read in Romans 1:18–20, people can see the evidence of a Creator within Creation—isn't that enough?

We see in the world around us a glimpse of God's power and authority, but those concepts lack direction or depth without the specific revelation of God's Word. In the Bible, we see not only God's work, but also the reasoning and purpose behind it. We see not only His might, but also His love—and the hope of a future with Him.

As Tozer wrote in the preface of his book:

> Sound Bible exposition is an imperative must in the Church of the living God. Without it no church can be a New Testament church in any strict meaning of that term. But exposition may be carried on in such way as to leave the hearers devoid of any true spiritual nourishment whatever. For it is not mere words that nourish the soul, but God Himself, and unless and until the hearers find God in personal experience, they are not the better for having heard the truth. The Bible is not an end in itself, but a means to bring men to an intimate and satisfying knowledge of God, that they may enter into Him, that they may delight in His Presence, may taste and know the inner sweetness of the very God Himself in the core and center of their hearts.

That is the goal of this chapter—and indeed this entire study: that you will know God and delight in His presence. As you do so, you'll find that He will transform your thoughts and your inner being to better reflect Him—which will lead you to seek Him even more.

. . . .

Student Work

Knowing God Involves a Personal Relationship

To truly know people, we must regularly interact with them. We learn not only by hearing what they have to say about themselves, but also by seeing them react and respond to various situations. We see them when they're happy, when they're sad, when they're angry—in every instance learning more about how they view the world and what exactly they value most.

And for us to say that we have a relationship, we must develop a *mutual* acquaintance with the other person—a two-way, face-to-face friendship. Friends are friends because they open up their thoughts and dreams to each other, then go through life with a shared awareness of each other's companionship.

As the teacher's lesson for this chapter pointed out, it is therefore important not only that we know God, but also that *He knows us*. Of course, being omniscient, God already knows everything about everyone. But He does not have a Father-child relationship with those who reject Christ.

- Read Matthew 7:21–23. According to these verses, is everyone who calls Jesus Lord actually part of His kingdom? _____

- Can people prove that they follow God by performing miracles or good works? _____

- What does God tell these people at the final judgment?

  _____

  _____

This gives rise to a question: "Whom does God know?"

- Read John 14:6–10. How must we approach God the Father?

  _____

- Who was the source of everything Jesus said on Earth?

  _____

To know Christ is to know God. He was and is completely, entirely *God in the flesh*, the living definition of love and truth. Only those who truly know Jesus truly know God.

God Is Holy

We face many challenges in knowing God. He is not only invisible, having chosen to reveal Himself through faith, but He is also holy, as we learned back in Chapter 1.

Read 1 Timothy 6:15–16. Here we find a terrific picture of God's holiness and transcendence. Note in particular verse 16. God's holiness is so fierce and pure that humans, in their physical, bodily form, could not even come close to His glory. This matches what we find in Exodus 33:20, when God told Moses that no one could see His face and survive. God instead revealed Himself in the Old Testament with signs of fire, wind, and smoke—supernatural events that communicated His power, but obscured the holiness that people could not yet know.

Humans Are Sinful

To complicate the matter further, we are by nature sinful. Our sin represents the opposite of holiness. Holiness is the manifest character of God, whereas sin is a rejection of everything He says is good and right. God's holiness *Job* does not allow sin anywhere close to it. The "anti-holy" cannot approach the holy, or the holy would no longer be so. God is God in part because no sin exists in His exalted presence.

✒ Read Isaiah 6:1–7. Why did the prophet Isaiah despair when he saw the throne of God?

_____

_____

But God in His grace forgave Isaiah, purging him of his sin (v. 7) and giving him a chance to declare God's message to His people.

In our sin, we could no more endure a moment in the exalted presence of God than a piece of tissue paper could survive a minute in a blazing furnace.

Christ Is the Mediator

Christ serves as the bridge to our holy God.

✒ Note 1 Timothy 2:5–6. What does verse 5 call Christ? _____

✒ Look up this word in a dictionary. How is the term defined?

_____

_____

_____

_____

✒ According to verse 6, how then did Christ serve in this role?

_____

_____

✒ He sacrificed Himself to pay the price for our sin. According to Colossians 1:20–22, He did this to reconcile us to God—and then present us to God in what way (v. 22)?

_____

_____

35

When we accept Christ as our Savior, He restores our relationship with God, bridging the chasm caused by sin and enabling us to know God—imperfectly, for now, yet still intimately, like a small child can know and trust a parent.

Knowing God Involves Personal Fellowship

As the teacher's lesson explained, Christ gives us a relationship with God, but that is just the first step in knowing Him. A person born or adopted into a family is just as much a family member as anyone else—yet it takes years of personal fellowship for those people to truly know and love each other well. An infant does not know his parents as well as a teenager, and a teenager does not know his parents as well as an adult who has endured the same kind of struggles and hardship.

In the same way, we can say that, right after the moment of our salvation, we know God. But it takes years of study, years of answered prayer, years of grace through hardship, and years of delight and communion before that knowledge grows up, flowers, and bears fruit.

How then do we grow in our knowledge of God? Well, in one sense, He does the growing *for* us. Remember, just as we can't save ourselves, neither can we make ourselves holy. But God also does not force us to fellowship with Him. He reveals Himself to us as we choose to abide in Him, and that abiding can include the following activities.

Through a Meaningful Prayer Life

In the Old Testament, God made His presence known to the people of Israel by a cloud of smoke that rested over His tabernacle. The same kind of sign appeared in some of the temples that followed in later years, but it was hidden behind a thick fabric veil in a room called the Holy of Holies. The Law prescribed how and when a priest could enter this chamber—usually just once a year, and only after rituals that symbolized deep purification.

But when Jesus talked with the Samaritan woman in John 4, He explained that people would soon worship God directly—not in a temple, but in spirit and in truth. They could commune with God wherever they were, and God's presence would reveal itself wherever His Spirit rested in the hearts of His children.

That's why, when Christ died on the cross, the veil in Herod's Jerusalem Temple ripped open, from top to bottom. No longer would God interact with humanity merely through rituals and symbols, but through direct, personal fellowship.

✏ Read Hebrews 10:19–22. Because of Christ's sacrifice, where can we now go (v. 19)? _____

✏ And how does verse 22 describe the purification that allows us to enter this place?

_____

_____

_____

_____

_____

What once was represented by physical purification is now a spiritual reality for all Christians. Christ has washed away our sin, and we can draw close to God by speaking directly with Him.

✏ Read Hebrews 4:14–16. How does this passage say we can approach God's throne of grace? _____

✏ And as we approach His throne in prayer, what does He give us?

_____

_____

Through prayer we know God more intimately. As we unload the burdens of our hearts, and as He responds to our prayers with the help we need, we learn more of His kindness, grace, and mercy.

Do you approach God with boldness, confident that He will provide you everything you need (Phil. 4:19)? Or do you speak to Him out of duty or obligation, as if He were an aging relative you visited out of routine, rather than love? Do you understand how much you need Him—how much you depend on this relationship for your spiritual well-being? Do you enjoy Him, or do you harbor unconfessed sin in your heart?

Through a God-Centered Reading of the Bible

In previous chapters, we learned that we do not merely study the Word—but God through His Word. When we seek Him, He draws close to us (James 4:8). Through reading His Word we see His power, love, omniscience, faithfulness, and a thousand other qualities and attributes, some of which we'll examine in later chapters.

Through Difficulties

Psalm 119:65–72 illustrates the goodness of God even in difficult times of life.

✎ What was David's condition *before* he was afflicted—that is, before he endured suffering (v. 67)? _____

✎ What did his affliction cause him to do (v. 67, 71)?

_____

_____

✎ And what did he learn from the Scriptures (v. 68)?

_____

_____

As Christ taught His disciples in John 9:1–3, not every trouble we face in this life results from our sin. Some troubles, like the persecution faced by David, exist to encourage us to depend on God, who is the Giver of every good and perfect gift (James 1:17). We need Him always, regardless of whether we think we're having a rough time.

But in all things, we can be confident that God is working for our good (Rom. 8:28). That doesn't mean we seek out trouble for its own sake. As Paul wrote in 1 Timothy 2:2, we should prefer a quiet and peaceful life. And we shouldn't needlessly endure abuse, either. As stewards of God's image in us, we should remove ourselves from people who cause us serious harm. Like David, we should trust God and honor authorities, but we should also dodge javelins (1 Sam. 18:11), make known the dangers to other authorities, and flee to a safer place with people we can trust.

And like David, we can record and recount God's work in our lives. Here a notebook or journal can be helpful, one that includes struggles, requests, and examples of God's faithfulness. Such a record can, over the years, remind us and teach us of God's goodness.

Challenge

What is your *relationship* to God? Do you still reject Christ, or have you accepted His sacrifice for you? If you have not yet depended on Jesus for your salvation, you can do so now. Simply trust what He did on the cross as payment for your sins—sins that you should now reject. And recognizing that you can do nothing to save yourself, ask Christ to redeem you into God's family.

What about your *fellowship* with God? Do you seek Him in His Word? Do you listen to what He says? Do you think about what you find, carefully, critically, and with an attitude of devotion?

Do you depend on God through prayer? Or do you allow sin to distract you (Ps. 66:18)? Confess your sin, and abide with God.

. . . .

Notes from the Teacher's Lesson

Knowing God—What It Isn't

- Knowledge about _____ (John 5:39–40)

- Knowledge about _____ (2 Tim. 3:1–5)

- Perfect knowledge of _____ (Isa. 55:9; Rom. 11:33; Eph. 3:19)

Knowing God—What It Is

- A personal _____ (Matt. 11:27)

- A personal _____ (2 Cor. 3:18)

Application Activities

1. Read Chapter 4 of Tozer's *The Pursuit of God.* Using Tozer's ideas as a starting point, define in your own words what it means to be "otherworldly." How does such a mindset affect our hopes, thoughts, and actions? Are there drawbacks to such a perspective? Write three or more paragraphs.

2. Write a short essay explaining how we can know God better through each of the following:

   A. Praying
   B. Studying Scripture
   C. Hearing the Word taught and preached
   D. Interacting with fellow believers
   E. Enduring hardship

3. List three things you have wondered about God. What doesn't make sense? What don't you understand? Keep these items in your notes, and as you learn more about God throughout this study, jot down any verses or insights that help you understand Him better.

   God is bigger than our questions and our doubts. The limitations in our understanding do not trouble Him—nor should they trouble us too much. But we can still seek Him in His Word, learn from the insights of mature believers, and trust Him to reveal His wisdom in His timing.

4. Choose one of the following, and explain how such a focus could corrupt our study of the Bible. What are the dangers of such a perspective?

   • "I'm looking for verses to prove my ideas correct."
   • "I want to learn more about King David. He's the perfect role model for me."
   • "I'm looking for verses that tell me the exact words I should pray."

thou shalt enlarge my

33 Teach me, O LORD, the way of thy statutes; and I shall keep it unto the end.

34 Give me understanding, and keep thy law; yea, I shall observe my whole heart.

35 Make me to go in the path commandments; for therein do I d

36 Incline my heart unto thy testimonies, and not to covetousness.

37 Turn away mine eyes from ing vanity; and quicken way

38 Stablish thy word un who is devoted to thy fear.

39 Turn away my reproach fear: for thy judgments are goo

40 Behold, I have longed af cepts: quicken me in thy rig

41 Let thy mercies come O LORD, even thy salvatio

CHAPTER 4

Meditating on God in His Word

"This blessed Book will fill your head with knowledge, and your heart with grace."

—Thomas Watson, *A Body of Divinity*

Rev. Samuel D. Lougheed was a chaplain in the Union Army during the U.S. Civil War, serving with the 8th Missouri Infantry during the Vicksburg campaign, when Major General Ulysses S. Grant successfully split the Confederacy in half. Before and after the war, Lougheed presided over a small Methodist congregation in Beaver Creek, Illinois, reaching out to his community along with his wife, Jennie.

Samuel and Jennie wrote frequently to each other during the war, though not as often as Samuel would have liked. He would despair whenever his wife's letters failed to reach him, and he assumed that she had forsaken him. In a few of his own letters, he would call her "cruel" and "heartless" for neglecting him—and then immediately apologize when he received her next letter. He often forgot about the unreliability of the wartime mail system.

In a way, Lougheed's discouragement was understandable. He saw much in the war that traumatized him. After the Battle of Shiloh, which left 23,000 soldiers dead, wounded, or missing, Lougheed helped bury dozens of bodies in mass graves. Between battles, he endured the worst of conditions, struggling to serve his men while keeping disease and hunger at bay. Most of the men in his regiment ignored his preaching—occupying themselves with drinking and gambling—and Lougheed could understand why. "Sometimes, I think," he wrote, "What reward has the man who keeps sober?"

Within a year of service, any romantic sentiment Lougheed could have had about the war was gone. While he remained committed to the Union's cause, he despaired to think that God could bless his regiment, which he felt represented the worst of humanity. The officers opposed his attempts to hold services. The soldiers often looted or stole what they wanted. Nine men in the regiment even assaulted a young civilian woman.

As Lougheed wrote in December, 1862*:

> I know God is able to make the wrath and wickedness of men serve Him, and my prayer is that He will do it. But, my dear, I am now fully converted to the belief that if we are dealt with as we deserve we must suffer defeat, and our enemies triumph over the nation, and the last hopes of humanity in relation to republican institutions must be forever entombed. But O Lord, have mercy upon our wicked, our Christ-less army. And for the sake of the few who do fear Thee, give success to our arms, and hasten the time when the nation shall learn war no more.

Little sustained Lougheed except for his time with the Scriptures and the grace he saw in his wife's letters.

> My Dear Precious Wife,
>
> For one week or more I have felt sad and sick. Sad, because I could not hear from you—day after day passed, and nothing, no nothing could I hear. Well, my sadness broke away today like the storm cloud in a summer sky when God throws the rainbow over it. Just so with your letter. Had it been your own sweet self, whispering words of gentleness and kindness upon my spirit, the dispelling of the cloud of gloom which hung over my mind, could not have been more apparent.

Samuel cherished Jennie's letters, reading them over and over by candlelight because he longed for the day he could return to his family.

> My home is to me the brightest, happiest spot on Earth. It is there my own dear Jennie is the presiding angel. There too are my own

*Excerpts taken from the Samuel P. Lougheed Letters, University of Washington Special Collections.

sweet children, of whom, with thee Love, ever, I'm fondly thinking no matter where I may roam. Tis near thee, and my dear children, I desire to live.

And whenever, or wherever, it is my lot to die, I ask with my last gasp to lisp the precious names of Jesus, Jennie, and my children, and there let me repose in silence, till we all meet again, Love, ne'er to sever, on the other side of Jordan in the sweet fields of Eden, where the tree of life is blooming.

Sweet hope; sweet prospect, sweet Heaven. Then, Love, life's voyage will be over. Life's cares, anxieties, and toils will all be ended. Our hopes and fears will too forever cease; for we then will realize the full fruition of the things hoped for during our state of probation. The things we saw so faintly through faith's dim eye, on Earth, we will then behold with unobstructed vision.

. . . I expect I shall see the blessed Jesus, I shall look for the prints of the nails in His precious hands and feet, I shall look for the side opened by the soldier's spear, I shall look also for the scars made in His sacred temples during the terrible battle of Calvary, where the Captain of our salvation was wounded, and pierced many times, but was ultimately the Victor, and triumphed over every foe. I shall want to kiss His hallowed feet, and shout His praises as loudly as the angels will let me, and as long as the endless ages last.

After the fall of Vicksburg, Lougheed returned to his wife and children in Illinois. In his absence, Jennie had continued Samuel's ministry and maintained the family farm, but they would soon move west, first to Kansas and then to Washington, where Samuel died in 1893 at the age of 68.

In Lougheed's letters we find the heights of hope and the depths of despair— places we can all reach as we walk the path God gives us. But like this discouraged chaplain, we should look in hope to the words written by the One who loves us most.

God's Word is full of the love and grace that we need during our long journey through this hard and often disheartening world. Around us we see wickedness and despair—and even good causes falling ruin to horrible people. But in the

Scriptures we find perfect truth, truth worth fighting toward, truth worth clinging to in faith until we see God's face with our own eyes.

. . . .

Student Work

Review

Using your notes from the first three chapters, answer the following questions.

✎ For what purpose did God create us? _____

✎ In 1 Peter 1:16, what does God call us to be? _____
This is perhaps the most important way we can glorify God.

✎ Knowing God involves what two things?

- A personal _____ Relationship _____ with God

- A personal _____ fellowship _____ with God

Meditation

The Definition of Godly Meditation

Godly meditation occurs when we focus our thoughts on God's character and work. This is a purposeful activity—something that takes discipline, but something that we pursue out of a love for our God. Many Christians will let the Bible dictate what they do and what they say, but not everyone lets the knowledge of God infuse their core thinking.

In a way, we're all meditation experts—we're always thinking about *something*. But it takes effort to train ourselves to focus on the right things—to look at God, others, and ourselves the way we should, and to dwell on His truth, not our fears and failures.

✎ Read Psalm 63:1. Describe David's longing for God, as shown in this verse.

_____

_____

_____

As we read in Psalm 119, David delighted in meditating on God's Word—but only because he delighted in the God of the Word. He cherished these "love letters" because he cherished the God of Love who sent them. This God deserves David's thoughts and attention.

The Steps of Meditation

Following is a suggested method of meditation you can apply to your daily devotions. The steps shown here represent a rough path along which you can approach God purposefully and fruitfully.

Prepare

Find a good time and place to simply *be* with God.

🖊 Read Psalm 63:6. When and where did David choose to think about God?

_____

_____

🖊 Read each of the following passages as well, noting when the people spent time thinking about God's truth.

- Psalm 1:2 – _At night._
- Joshua 1:8 – _Midiate day and night._
- Genesis 24:63 – _At the field._
- Deuteronomy 11:18–19 –
  talk to family and people about God.

_____

_____

Like Isaac, you could go to meditate in a field, or, like Christ, you could pray alone in the wilderness (Luke 5:16). In either case, find a place of relative solitude and quiet, even if you don't have a field, mountain, or desert nearby. And you needn't use a literal closet like the one Christ suggested in Matthew 6:6, but you should be alone enough that the distractions and concerns of other people do not intrude into your thoughts.

Collect

Gather in front of you truth that you can read and cherish. You might not actually tie bundles of Scripture to your forehead—like the Israelites' frontlets in Deuteronomy 11:18—but you should select a passage or collection of verses to guide your thoughts.

You might simply have an open Bible, or you might have a stack of flashcards that feature verses to encourage and challenge you.

Rehearse

One key tool to aid your memory is repetition.

Why? Because the human brain contains around 100 billion neurons, each of which communicates with its neighbors by building thousands of synaptic connections. These pathways can convey, modulate, or amplify a bio-electric signal in less than 0.002 seconds—allowing for waves of repeatedly firing neurons that result in the phenomena of human consciousness and thought.

And as two neurons—or two clusters of neurons—communicate over and over again, the connection between them grows stronger. New bridges may form, either through long, tube-like *axons* or short, branched *dendrites*. Over time, the brain alters itself so that thoughts requiring these high-traffic connections are *physically easier* to think.

In short, the more you think something, the easier it is to think it. The more you reinforce a certain pattern of thought, the more that pattern will link to other areas of thought. A path of thought may become so deeply engrained in your brain that it's almost impossible *not* to think. That's a danger for evil or self-abusive thoughts, but a blessing for thoughts that reflect God's own.

✎ What phrase is repeated 26 times in Psalm 136? This was meant as a chorus that a congregation could repeat as a priest recited the goodness of God.

His love endures forever

It's helpful to read a single passage of Scripture over and over again in one sitting. The first reading might seem interesting; the second time might be a chore; and the third might feel like a waste of time. But by the fourth or fifth reading, you'll discover that you can follow the theme and scope of the text, you'll remember its truth that much better, and you'll likely notice details and meaning you never saw before.

Connect

Another way to improve your memory is to connect the truth you're learning to other truths. The more "paths" you build between ideas, the more you can remember them all together.

As we see in Psalm 136, God revealed His love and mercy through Creation, through the preservation of Israel, and through countless other works.

List four specific examples of God's glory and goodness in Psalm 136.

The moon and stars to govern the night — verses 9.
in the goodness of him.
In the people we don't like,
we see it through his word

Like the congregants who might sing this psalm together, we should take a single truth about God and look for different ways in which it is expressed.

For each truth you consider in meditation, ask yourself the following:

- How does this truth enhance my understanding of God?
- Where else do I see this truth in Scripture? Pillipians 1:6
- How can this truth affect the way I view myself?
- How can this truth affect the way I view and treat others?

Not only will this activity reinforce your faith, but it will also sharpen your understanding. A person who looks for examples of God's love in Scripture will have a much more precise understanding of what love truly looks like. Instead of fitting God into your own definition of love, you should refine your definition of love around God.

Record

Take time also to record your thoughts and discoveries in a daily journal.

🖊 Read Joshua 4:1–7. Why did God instruct the people of Israel to make a pile of stones near the Jordan River?

_____

_____

_____

_____

It's worth recording the work of God in your life. To better appreciate His love over time, you could briefly write the following for each day:

- **Reading** – Today's passage of Scripture
- **Focus** – The focus of your meditation
- **Thoughts** – Key thoughts that arose during your meditation
- **Questions** – The burdens, doubts, and questions that you shared with God
- **Answers** – The answers to prayer that you saw most recently
- **Praises** – Examples of other ways you believe God is working in your life

Praise

Even in the most difficult times of life, our response to God's character and work should be praise. As we think on God's truth, we wonder at why He'd share such grace with us. And as we think on God's love, we cannot help but be grateful for the sacrifice of His Son.

Take time to thank God for Who He is and what He's done—praising Him also for the hope we have to one day be with Him.

Challenge

🖊 Read Romans 11:33–12:2. According to verse 2, to what should our minds *not* conform? _____

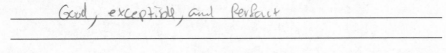 As God renews our mind and transforms us into a better image of Himself, what can we better see (v. 2)?

_____Good, exceptible, and Perfect_____

_____

Pursue God first. Sacrifice your time to meditate on Him through His Word, and watch how He'll work in you. Think on what you've learned, and take God's truth and love with you wherever you go.

. . . .

Notes from the Teacher's Lesson

The Instruments of Meditation

- God's _Creation_
- God's _Word_

The Focus of Meditation

- God's _Character_
- God's _Word_
- God's _Creation_

The Importance of Meditation

- Our thoughts naturally _Our sinful_ (Rom. 7:15–20).

- God's thoughts are _Pure / good_ (Isa. 55:8–9).

- Through meditation God blesses us . . .
  - With _understanding_ (Ps. 119:97–100)
  - With _awe / response_ (Ps. 77:12; 145:5)
  - With _Fruitfulness_ (Ps. 1)
  - With _Honor_ (Ps. 8:3–5; 19:14; 104:34)

Application Activities

1. Read and meditate on Psalm 19. Rehearse the passage in your mind at least five times, and record your thoughts. Draw a picture that can remind you of the truths taught in this psalm.

2. Using a reputable Bible concordance or online resource, list at least five examples of metaphors, symbols, or imagery used to describe God's Word. For example, Jeremiah 23:29 says that God's Word is both a fire and a hammer. Write out the reference and text for each example, along with a brief description of what you think the imagery means. Note: your teacher might help you identify reputable sources.

3. During the Civil War, whenever Samuel Lougheed did not receive a letter from his wife, he would often doubt her love for him—much like we can doubt God's love when we fail to see His hand at work. Imagine that you're Jennie, and write a reply to one of Samuel's letters. How would you correct him or encourage him? If you need inspiration, read some of Samuel's letters at the website for the University of Washington Special Collections.

4. Review the following suggestions by Thomas Watson to get the most from your Bible reading. Pick at least three of them, and write a paragraph about each one, explaining why you believe the suggestion could be helpful. If you believe that an item could be altered to better reflect something you find in Scripture, include a better suggestion, as well.

   A. Remove hindrances.
   B. Prepare your heart.
   C. Read with reverence.
   D. Persevere in remembering what you read.
   E. Meditate on what you read.
   F. Read it with an honest heart.
   G. Pay as much attention to its commands as to its promises.
   H. Pay particular attention to the examples and lives of the people in the Bible as living sermons.
   I. Don't stop reading until you feel your heart warmed.
   J. Put into practice what you read.

E.] -listen to christian music only
   - (Mis) Minister more often
   - Devotions continue everyday

F.] - Be honest with yourself and God.
   - Don't pretend that nothing is wrong.

J.] - help people
   - Pray
   - Real bible.

CHAPTER 5

Recognizing God's Providence

". . . nothing comes to pass but what is ordained by God's decree, and ordered by His providence."

—Thomas Watson, *A Body of Divinity*

Staggering from the wreckage of his racecar, the driver leaned shakily on the shoulder of the reporter who held a microphone to his face.

"How'd you manage to escape that collision without a scratch?" the reporter asked, nodding at her cameraman to get a closer shot. Behind them, ambulances and fire crews were cleaning up what remained of a fourteen-car pileup.

"I don't know," the driver answered, shaking his head. "I guess I got lucky."

- Or, "I guess I was thinking positive thoughts."
- Or, "I guess this charm here kept my angel close by."
- Or, "I guess fate wasn't done with me."
- Or, "I guess I decided that I had more to live for."
- Or, "I guess God thought I deserved to live a little longer."

"Oh," said the reporter. "But what about the driver behind you? It looks like the medics are carting him to the hospital."

"I guess it wasn't his day. You know, we all go out there on the track not knowing what'll happen. Whatever or whoever smiled down on me must not have cared about him, I guess."

We live in a world characterized by chaos. Since the fall of humanity, sin has cursed us with pain, conflict, and death—all of which affect us without apparent reason or cause.

Yet Christians, redeemed by Christ to live free from the bondage of sin and judgment, can see a different force behind the events and circumstances of our lives. We see God's providence—that is, the way He governs His entire Creation.

Nothing occurs outside of His knowledge. Even the hairs of our head are numbered (Matt. 10:30), and not a sparrow falls that God does not know (Matt. 10:29). From the tiniest of things God weaves a tapestry that includes the entire scope of history—the rise and fall of empires, the birth and death of cultures, the success and failure of revolutions, the debates and conflicts and wars that seem petty compared to the God that stands above Time itself. He guides the hearts of rulers however He wants (Prov. 21:1), and He directs history to its inevitable conclusion, where all of Creation will recognize His majesty.

As Thomas Watson wrote,

> There is no such thing as blind fate, but there is a providence that guides and governs the world. . . . [It] reaches to all places, persons, and occurrences.
>
> . . . Learn quietly to submit to divine providence. Do not murmur at things that are ordered by divine wisdom. We may no more find fault with the works of providence than we may with the works of creation. It is a sin as much to quarrel with God's providence as to deny His providence.

In this chapter, we consider the role of providence as a way to seek and know God more intimately.

. . . .

Student Work

Providence in Scripture

The Bible exists to showcase God's glory, so in Scripture we find numerous examples of God orchestrating the lives of men and women to reveal His love and truth in them. Let's review just a few.

Joseph

As you've probably read elsewhere, Joseph, the son of Jacob, endured horrific trials throughout his young life. His jealous brothers sold him into slavery, and the wife of his slavemaster accused him of sexual assault and had him imprisoned. Despite all his hard work, his situation seemed to get worse and worse. But God blessed him, finally setting him in a position within Pharaoh's court that allowed him to care for his family and save them from starvation.

✐ Read Genesis 50:15–21. What did Joseph's brothers do after their father died?

_____

_____

✐ And how did Joseph respond (vv. 19–21)?

_____

_____

_____

Through Joseph, we see a kind of grace and patience we rarely find in either Scripture or the rest of history. He could say what he did, not because he forgot about his brothers' sin or because they deserved to be forgiven, but because Joseph understood that God had worked in his life.

Rahab

Rahab was a prostitute living in Jericho, a fortress city in Canaan that God ordered the people of Israel to destroy before settling in the area. Joshua sent two spies to survey the city, and they lodged at the house of Rahab (Josh. 2:1).

✐ Read Joshua 2:8–16. How did God use Rahab to help the two spies?

_____

_____

_____

_____

✐ According to Hebrews 11:31, what motivated her help?

_____

Given what Rahab had heard about God's power, she feared Him. Nevertheless, she trusted that He would take care of those who clung to Him. She risked her life to save these two men and thereby demonstrated her faith in Jehovah. She would later marry an Israelite and become a direct ancestor of Christ—and stand as one of the greatest examples of God's grace in the Bible.

The Scriptures feature too many other stories to list, but here are a few:

- Ruth, whom God brought to Israel through the misfortunes and deaths in Naomi's family (Ruth 1:1–18)

- Solomon, whose parents only met because of an immoral, even murderous affair (2 Sam. 11)

- Daniel, whose ministry in Babylon only occurred because he and his friends were enslaved and put to service in a foreign country (Dan. 1:1–7)

- Esther, who became queen and saved her people after she survived the harem of King Ahasuerus (Esther 2:1–18)

- Aquila and Priscilla, who became an important part of Paul and Apollos' ministry, but only after they were expelled from Rome with the other Jewish refugees (Acts 18:1–4; 24–26)

Not every providence of mercy or misfortune is explained in the Bible, nor should we assume that we know God's specific reason for every event in our lives. Some good things happen to bad people, and many bad things happen to good people (Matt. 5:45). But we can trust that God is working through it all, both for our good and for His glory (Rom. 8:28). One day He will give us a perfect understanding of His work. acts 17:

Providence in Your Life

Take some time to reflect on your life thus far. Answer each question as your memory allows. Since some of the following information may be personal, you'll want to store it in a safe place. If you don't have a way to keep your answers private, don't write them down here, but do consider each question and, if possible, write your answers in a private journal or document.

✎ Name _Olena Hartzler_

✎ Birthdate _May 30, 2001_   Birthplace _Poroshkovo, Ukraine_

✎ Parents or Guardians _Stan and Julie Hartzler_

✎ Siblings
_Maria, Misha, Alina, looda, Angela, Vasa, Vania
Ulia,_

✎ My first memory
_I went to my dad's mom's house, there my mom
was being beaten by my dad, and I was trying to
walk, but I fell._

✎ How I'd describe my childhood
_I would describe my childhood as a very hard life.
I say that because I witness people being tortured,
I was tortured by people, I was beaten, raped, and
abused, I always got emotionally hurt, because my mom would
always be beaten by dad, because he gets drunk._

✎ My happiest memory from that time
_My birth mom hanging out with me and conficting
me._

✎ The worst hurt I've ever felt
When my dad tried to kill me.

✎ As I look back on that time, how can I see that God prepared me for what I face now?

God has prepared me in many different ways, such as he helps me to encourage people that went through the same events I did.

✎ And on the other hand—what is unclear? What did God allow to happen that still doesn't make sense?

I don't understand why he took me away from my birth family.

✎ What do I enjoy doing? What am I good at?

I enjoy helping people.
I enjoy writing poems and music.

✎ How do I most enjoy helping other people?

I enjoy helping them with there struggles

✎ What kind of person do I want to be? What do I want to do with my life?

I want to be a kind, and loving person
I also want to be a God like women.
I want to help people in millitary
I also want to be a missionary, China, N. Korea, India.

✎ Why do I have these desires? Did God give them to me? And if so, what might the reason be?

I think I know how it feels to be hurt so I can help people

✒ How I accepted Christ as Savior—that is, how He redeemed me to Himself:

Date Dec 25, 2011   Place   home

I was asking my mom ?'s and
         than I asked Jesus into
my heart.

✒ What other significant decisions have I made since then? How has Christ grown and changed me?

I chose what I want to do with my
life, he has given me a big heart.

✒ What things in my life now most concern me?

to helping People.

✒ Who or what can I trust to help and encourage me? What lifelines do I have?

hannah, Anna, lauren, Grandma, friends

✒ Should I find new sources of strength? If so, where should I look?

to Christ, in friends, bible.

✐ With what Bible character do I most identify? What person in Scripture faced challenges or opportunities similar to mine?

Job, or Joseph, because life is hard for me.

✐ In what way did God use that person to reveal His love and truth?

he has shown me that he works all things for good.

If you've answered all of the preceding questions, you have begun to meditate on God's providence in your life.

Hopefully you can begin to see God's hand in the events and circumstances of your life. As we are mindful of His work, we can be thankful for the blessings we've received—and also acknowledge the hardship we've suffered.

God never designed the Christian life to be lived alone, so if many of these memories are painful to write, please consider reaching out to a mature Christian that you can trust—one who can listen to your experiences and help you seek grace, hope, and joy. Particularly, if you've suffered—or are currently suffering—from physical, sexual, or emotional abuse, seek help *immediately* from someone you can trust, and do not stop seeking help until you feel safe from further harm. A parent, teacher, pastor, or civil official should refer you to people who can help you process your past and secure your future. Some hardships should be endured, but some should be escaped—for our own good, and for our ability to serve God without fear.

Challenge

Consider the words of John Flavel, a Puritan writer from the 1600s:

> O, is your life such a continued throng, such a mad hurry that there is no time for Christians to sit alone and think on these things, and press these marvelous manifestations of God in His providences upon their own hearts?

I cannot but judge it the concern of Christians that have time and ability for such a work, to keep written memorials or journals of Providence by them. . . .

If Christians in reading the Scriptures would judiciously collect and record the providences they shall meet with there, and (if destitute of other helps) but add those that have fallen out in their own time and experience, O what precious treasure would these make! What an antidote would it be to their souls against the spreading atheism of these days, and satisfy them beyond what many other arguments can do, that "The Lord, he is the God; the Lord, he is the God" (1 Kings 18:39).

Do not trust your slippery memories with such a multitude of remarkable passages of Providence as you have, and shall meet with in your way to heaven.

Take heed of clasping up those rich treasures in a book, and thinking it enough to have noted them there; but have frequent recourse to them, as oft as new needs, fears or difficulties arise and assault you. . . . Make it as much your business to preserve the sense and value as the memory of former providences, and the fruit will be sweet to you.

Notes from the Teacher's Lesson

What Is Providence?

- Providence includes _____ in our lives.

- Providence is the work of _____ (Ps. 47:2).

- Providence exists for _____ and _____ (Rom. 8:28).

Meditating on God Through Providence

- Biblical examples of meditating on providence:

    - The meditation of _____
      (Exo. 17:14–15; Josh. 4:1–7)

    - The meditation of _____ (Ps. 70)

    - The meditation of _____ (1 Sam. 1:20)

- The blessings of meditating on providence

    ○ Not everything depends on _____.

    ○ We can never fall outside _____
      (Jer. 29:11; Phil. 1:6).

    ○ We can view circumstances from a _____
      perspective.

    ○ We can _____ God's work with others.

- Tips for meditating on providence:

    ○ Consider the _____ of God's providence.

    ○ Consider the _____ of God's providence.

    ○ Consider the _____ of God's providence.

    ○ Consider providence that reflects _____
      from Scripture.

    ○ Consider _____,
      as revealed by His providence.

Application Activities

1. For one week—or one month, if your teacher prefers—keep a journal of providences, in which you record the ways you see God work in your daily life.

2. List and explain three examples of what you believe to be God's providence in your home country's history. Write one paragraph for each example.

3. Explain and evaluate the following statement in light of Scripture: "For the believer, there are no accidents." Limit your writing to three paragraphs.

4. Read the first chapter of William S. Plummer's book *Jehovah–Jireh: A Treatise on Providence*. Note the extra-biblical quotations listed under "Providence Asserted." Choose one of these quotes and write a short essay evaluating it in light of Scripture. Would you refine the quotation to better reflect God's truth?

5. Select a character in the Bible and produce an illustrated story of God's work in his or her life. Use at least seven illustrations.

End times

Amillenialism
- No Kingdom
- beilievers don't escape trials

Pre-millenialism
— Crist will return and rainfor 1000 years
- Jews will turn to christ (rom 10)
- Temple

Post millinalism
- beleivers make world better.

Rapture
— mid tribulation
— Final Judgement

CHAPTER 6

The Priorities of One Who Knows God

"Aim purely at God's glory. We do this when we prefer God's glory above all other things; above credit, estate, relations; when the glory of God coming in competition with them, we prefer His glory before them."

—Thomas Watson, *A Body of Divinity*

We're all busy, whether we serve as students, parents, businesspeople, pastors, or teachers. Those who succeed in any one area, however, do so because they learn to establish priorities, focusing their time and effort on a few things to the exclusion of others. Many plan out their "big picture" and set goals to finish what they believe to be important. A violinist, for instance, might practice his art instead of playing basketball with his friends. And a runner hits her route at sunup, while the rest of her friends are still sleeping.

In economics, you may have learned about the concept of *opportunity cost*. Everything you do costs you more than time—it also costs you whatever else you could have done with that same time, money, or energy. With a billion good things to do, and only one lifetime to do them all, we have to prioritize. We have to choose what is most important, and we can't let our choices get buried under the avalanche of activities and distractions we see in this world.

Many of us just have too many irons in the fire at once. We busy ourselves with too many things, thereby ensuring that we do nothing really well. If you can't list your priorities in ten to fifteen seconds, it's likely that you don't have any.

Some people, however, do take time to set priorities, but they're unworthy priorities. They might chase wealth, prestige, or some vague idea of happiness. But while those things can be good, they're not worth pursuing in and of themselves. As Christ taught His disciples in Matthew 6:33, we should seek first the kingdom of God, and trust Him to add these other wants and needs to our life as He sees fit.

As we set proper priorities, we should concern ourselves with both *efficiency* and *effectiveness*. Efficiency is doing something with the right amount of time and effort. It's working smart, not hard. Effectiveness, on the other hand, is doing something *well*—meeting the goals you've set and fulfilling your responsibilities to others. If we force ourselves to set priorities, we discipline ourselves to be good stewards of God's gifts and serve Him the best that we can.

Set your goals and standards high. Learn how to succeed, and just as importantly, learn how best to respond to failure. Laugh a little at your slip-ups when you can, and trust God to continue using you. Take your responsibilities seriously—and your ego not so much.

Part of maturity is discovering who you are and what gifts God gave you. Work *with* your strengths and *around* your weaknesses, and ask God to help you be who you are even as He molds you into someone better.

Review

Answer the following questions, consulting your notes as necessary.

✏ In what ways do we glorify God?

School, life, relationships, and body / words.

✏ Through what specific activity does this study suggest that we turn knowledge *about* God into knowledge *of* God? _Chennyl_

✏ Through what two main instruments do we pursue this activity?

Prayer / bible

✐ List the six steps for this activity, as offered by Chapter 4.

- _day   Review_
- _night   Meditation_
- _field_
- _life_
- _words_
- _body_

✐ Write the five tips for this activity given in Chapter 5.

- _God's work_
- _Our work_
- _Spirits work_
- _Son's work_
- _my parents work._

. . . .

Notes from the Teacher's Lesson

Priority One: Our Relationship with _God_
(Luke 14:25–28; Matt. 6:25–34)

Priority Two: Our _Family_ *(1 Tim. 5:8)*

Priority Three: Our _Ministry to_ 🧍 *(2 Cor. 3:2–6)*

. . . .

Meditation Projects

Beginning with this lesson, your teacher may ask you to complete two additional projects each week.

- First, you will read an assigned passage of Scripture, recording everything you see of God's character as you meditate on those verses.

- Second, you will take the time to meditate on God's providence and record a few of your thoughts.

Project One – Meditation on God in Scripture

Read Psalm 105, and record the characteristics of God that you see in this chapter. This psalm reviews some of Israel's history while highlighting God's wondrous works:

- It begins by calling on God's people to *remember* His providence (vv. 1–6).

- Then it continues by calling attention to God's goodness in His covenant with Abraham (vv. 8–15), the lives of Joseph and Israel in Egypt (vv. 16–24), and in the life of Moses (vv. 25–38).

- Then the passage reviews God's care for Israel while they wandered the wilderness (vv. 39–41) and when they entered Canaan (vv. 42–45).

After carefully recording the things you learn about God in this chapter, give the sheet to your teacher. You may want to record more personal thoughts on a separate, private document.

Project Two

Each week, your teacher may ask you to meditate on one of four different categories of providence, as explained below.

- Biblical—Different figures from the Bible will be assigned during the year. Ponder the life of each person, and record what you see of God's character and God's work.

- Historical—For each event assigned to you, ponder how God may have moved in those circumstances to show people His love and truth.

- Contemporary—Consider also the ways that God works in the lives of those people you know. Record in this category the testimonies of other believers who are living now.

- Personal—This category includes all providence that you identify in your own life—that is, ways you experience God's work firsthand.

For each example of providence, record what you can of the following:

Date and Situation

Describe the event.

October 5, 2019. Car broke down near Sunset Way. Had a chance to talk to the tow truck driver about his family. After hearing him say he wanted better friends for his kids, I invited him to bring his family to our church's Wednesday night dinner. I briefly shared how God uses His people in my life.

What God Did

State how you believe God may have worked.

God orchestrated my meeting with the driver, and He brought up an opportunity to share about His work in my life.

Timing

Sometimes this is important to the providence.

Our car broke down when this driver was available and willing to chat for a while.

Forerunner Events

Describe the event that incited this story.

Our car broke down—not looking forward to the repair cost.

Tools

Note the person or things God used to work in your life—or to direct your attention to Him.

When the driver spoke about his family, I felt the need to offer a suggestion.

Promises Fulfilled

Note any Scripture that came to your mind—usually a promise, but also perhaps a warning or command.

I thought about our call to be "living epistles" (2 Cor. 3:2–6).

God's Character

Record every facet of God's character that you see in the situation.

God is sovereign—He protected us from a serious accident. God is generous—He will provide for the repair expense. God's Spirit moved the driver to open up to me.

Thoughts and Reflections

Record anything else that came to your mind, including how this experience might affect the way you approach similar situations in the future. What else specifically can you thank God for?

If your teacher doesn't provide you with another assignment, try an example of providence sometime back in your first ten years of life. Consider talking to your parents or guardians about any extraordinary event that occurred before you could remember—perhaps even at your birth. Ponder how this event might have brought you to where you are, and record what you can see of God's work.

Application Activities

1. Refer to the first Application Activity listed at the end of Chapter 1.

   • Review the goals you wrote down for each of the eight categories. By this point in your study, do you believe that you should revise any of your goals—or add new ones? Do your goals honor God, both individually and as a whole?
   • Make any necessary additions or adjustments, and then write down the steps you should take to reach each of these goals, including ways you can pursue those goals day by day, bit by bit. Where applicable, set a deadline for each goal.

2. List the names of several people whom you believe set godly priorities successfully.

   • Ask to meet with them, if possible, and interview them about how they arrived at their priorities.
   • Ask them what advice they would offer to young people who want to pursue similar work.
   • Write a brief summary of each interview.

3. Purchase or compile a weekly calendar.

   • Write the deadlines for your annual, monthly, and weekly goals.
   • Include deadlines also from your class syllabi.
   • Make weekly and daily to-do lists.
   • Set aside time to tackle large projects bit by bit.
   • Check off each item as you finish it.

4. For what would you most want to be remembered after you die? What should be the theme or legacy of your life? Using the following categories, list the things for which you'd like people to remember you:

   A. General accomplishments   C. Character traits

   B. Academic, professional, and creative achievements   D. Family life

   Then write out the steps you can take *today* to make each of those desires a reality, noting especially those areas in which you believe that you should change.

CHAPTER 7

The Characteristics of One Who Knows God

"Though the main work of religion lies in the heart, yet our light must so shine that others may behold it. The safety of a building is the foundation, but the glory of it is in the frontispiece; so the beauty of faith is in the conversation."

—Thomas Watson, *A Body of Divinity*

Successful people in every profession possess certain qualities or characteristics that have made them successful.

For example, the characteristics of a professional athlete likely include physical strength, stamina, speed, patience, good reflexes, self-discipline, mental alertness, and excellent hand-eye coordination. A successful businessperson must have knowledge of relevant products, services, markets, competition, as well as good financial skills and an ability to plan for future opportunities and problems before they arise.

Christians must develop specialized characteristics, skills, and disciplines, as well. We do not simply profess that God is God—we follow His leadership and reflect His goodness to others. Doing that well takes time, patience, and practice as God's Spirit works in and through us.

Our dependence on God affects every area of life. It affects the way we think—the way that we look at God, others, and ourselves. This, in turn, impacts our actions—the way we discipline ourselves and serve other people. Since we no longer live bound to the old system of sin and judgment, we are free to love and speak truth as Christ would.

Student Work

The teacher's lesson for this chapter discusses three broad characteristics of the person who knows God, as shown in Psalm 1. Many other specific qualities of godliness can be found listed in R. A. Torrey's book, *How to Succeed in the Christian Life*. Some of these are as follows:

- The open, public confession of Christ
- An assurance of salvation; a trust in God's work
- Committed fellowship in a body of believers
- Regular, consistent Bible study
- Active service for Christ
- A wise choice of close companions

The Application Activities for this chapter—and for those following—may help you develop these areas of your life.

✎ Read Colossians 1:28. Why did Paul proclaim and teach Christ?

_____

_____

_____

_____

Our goal is not merely to rejoice in the relationship we already have with God, but to walk with Him in greater wisdom and maturity.

✎ Read James 1:2–4 and 1 Peter 2:20–23. In your own words, explain a mature attitude toward suffering inflicted on us by others.

_____

_____

_____

_____

_____

_____

_____

_____

_____

✐ Read Romans 5:3–5. What sequence of growth is outlined in this passage?

_____

_____

_____

_____

_____

_____

Review

✐ List the three priorities of the person who knows God, as ordered in the previous lesson.

- _____

- _____

- _____

✐ Write the steps of meditation, as suggested by this study.

- _____

- _____

- _____

- _____

- _____

- _____

✐ On what three aspects of God should we focus our meditation?

- _____

- _____

- _____

✐ In your own words, what is a life message?

_____

_____

_____

_____

Notes from the Teacher's Lesson

The One Who Does Not Walk with the Wicked *(Ps. 1:1)*

The righteous person does not . . .

- ○ _____

- ○ _____

- ○ _____

The One Who Delights in God's Word *(Ps. 1:2; 119:103)*

The One Who Grows in God's Word *(Ps. 1:3; Jer. 2:12–13; 17:5–8)*

Spiritual success is . . .

- ○ _____

- ○ _____

Application Activities

1. Meditate on the Lord as revealed in Psalm 103. Record all of the things you see about Him in this chapter.

2. Continue meditating on the providences of God in the life of a contemporary. Ask a Christian you know for something that happened to them in the last five years that revealed God's goodness to them.

3. Read and report—either orally or in writing—on one of the following books. Your teacher may provide you with specific project guidelines or other book choices.

   - *How to Succeed in the Christian Life* by R. A. Torrey
   - *Spiritual Leadership* by J. Oswald Sanders
   - *Through Gates of Splendor* by Elisabeth Elliot
   - *The Screwtape Letters* by C. S. Lewis
   - *The Holiness of God* R. C. Sproul

4. Based on your study of the Word, briefly define spiritual *maturity* and spiritual *immaturity*—and list at least ten characteristics of each, perhaps in parallel. Ask God to help you identify one or more characteristics with which you need help, and list at least three passages from Scripture that will encourage you to better reflect His love and truth in that area.

UNIT 2
The Nature of God

"No man doth exactly know himself, much less doth he understand the full nature of a spirit; much less still the nature and perfection of God."

—Stephen Charnock, *The Existence and Attributes of God*

CHAPTER 8

A Spirit and a Person

"God is a Spirit . . . He gave us a spirit with one object of holding fellowship with Himself."

—Andrew Murray, *God's Best Secrets*

Philip grew up in a home that some people might call "troubled." His mother disappeared before he could remember, and while his father never hesitated to complain about her, Philip didn't completely understand what led to her departure.

Philip's father didn't beat him, but neither did Philip ever feel safe in the house. At times, his father would yell and break things, and at other times he would sulk about and give Philip the silent treatment. Philip almost preferred the yelling.

Philip and his sisters did go to a good church, however, usually accompanied by their father. People could see them all neatly dressed in a row, standing and singing and sitting and listening, each with a neatly bound Bible.

At home, Philip's father would review the sermon, picking out the points he thought emphasized Philip's failures. Philip did fail a lot, and his father was keen to remind him, often even shaming him in public for things he had done long ago, things he had already apologized for and made right. As much as the father seemed concerned about maintaining the family's reputation, he didn't mind trashing Philip's.

Philip's father was always angry—sometimes loudly, sometimes quietly. And though Philip wanted more than anything to please him, he could never meet his father's standards. His father never taught him to do better, nor did the man list all his unspoken rules—except when Philip broke them.

Consider Amy's family, however. Her father left her mother, Sharon, when Amy was five. And though Sharon still hurt from the separation, she showed Amy pictures of what once was a happy, unified family.

Sharon struggled to provide for her two children—Amy and her brother, Chris—but she had the support of a loving church family who could step in to provide childcare or even some financial help when needed.

Sharon was handy around the home, and she taught Amy and Chris how to use their father's old tools, which once gathered dust in the garage. One of Amy's proudest moments was when she surprised her mother with a wooden centerpiece made to look like a small flowerbed. It was rough around the edges, a little crooked, and the stain had dried funny, but Sharon set it proudly on their small dining table, and she didn't even put it away when some guests stayed for dinner.

Amy knew that Sharon wasn't perfect. As tough as their life was, it was easy to get discouraged, and sometimes Sharon didn't treat her children as lovingly as she should. But Amy always knew that she could bring her problems to her mother. If she felt any hesitation, it was because as she grew older, she didn't want to burden her mother unnecessarily. Yet Amy knew that Sharon depended on God for her joy and comfort, so Amy could, at least to some degree, depend on her.

Though we learn about God primarily through His Word, we cannot help but experience some of that knowledge with feelings we've developed toward our parents. Our fathers and mothers are often our first glimpses of God—in the sense that, like Him, they should love us, instruct us, and when necessary, correct us.

If you were Philip, how might you be tempted to think about God? As you read about His care and correction, what earthly reference point would you use?

And if you were Amy, how much different could your picture of God be? How could your mother's character help you better understand God?

Thankfully, our parents are not God—and God is not necessarily like our parents. It's important to keep our thoughts about one separate from the other. But we should recognize when our feelings toward our parents influence our feelings toward God, and we should seek God directly, growing in the knowledge of His Word and meditating on Him.

Student Work

How you view God will dictate every other belief and action. Your *theology*—your study of God—represents your highest and most important thoughts.

As A. W. Tozer wrote:

> The history of mankind will probably show that no people has ever risen above its religion, and man's spiritual history will positively demonstrate that no religion has ever been greater than its idea of God.

Every culture is built on its philosophy of life, and every philosophy is built on its conception of what is sacred, and every conception of the sacred is built on who people believe that God is.

If you know a person's theology—that is, what they think God is like—you can know a lot about how that person views the world in general. How we think about God determines . . .

- How we view ourselves
- How we view others
- How we act
- How we serve God
- What attitudes we have

If a person thinks he serves an angry, unloving God, he will live in fear and look at service as a matter of duty, not love. If a person thinks she serves an unholy, permissive God, she will do whatever she wants, coming to God in prayer only when she thinks she needs Him. If a person believes that there is no God, he will replace the idea with an ideal, a cause, or simply himself, and then devote his life to making his existence slightly less painful.

We must have a proper view of God. We must build our conception of Him on His Word.

So if we can't define God—as the teacher's lesson explains—what is God like? We might answer that question by saying that God is not exactly like anything—that is, He isn't reflected perfectly in any way by anything or anyone.

That is the glory of God—there is nothing that compares to Him. Note that in Scripture the prophets who tried to describe God made ample use of the word *like*.

✎ Read Ezekiel 1:4–14. How many times does the prophet use comparative language in his description of God? Count each instance of *like*, *likeness*, *appearance*, and similar terms.

_____

Ezekiel sees heaven opened, and he finds himself looking at a vision that mere words could not fully describe. The nearer he approaches the throne of God, the less sure his words become.

✎ In Ezekiel 1:26–28, he sees the glory of God Himself. Again, count and record the number of times he uses comparative language in this passage.

_____

Note that Ezekiel, in describing God, takes what is *not* God and uses it to help us visualize what He is *like*. Likewise, whatever we visualize God to be *cannot* be exactly correct, for we've built our conception of God out of things that are not Him. Ultimately, it's impossible to understand God fully until we see and know Him in person.

But while we're on this Earth, we can still study Him in the Word and in His providence.

Doctrines Dependent on Our Theology

What teachings does our study of God impact?

Doctrines of Salvation and Sanctification

Unless we somehow understand God to be holy, powerful, and just, we will not see ourselves as sinners, and we will not see our need to trust Christ.

✎ Read Isaiah 6. What part of the vision led Isaiah to declare himself a sinner?

_____

_____

_____

✎ Read John 3:16–17. What motive did God have to send Christ to the people of the world?

_____

_____

✎ Read Philippians 1:1–6. In the spirit of grace and peace, upon whom do we depend to become more holy (v. 6)? _____

Doctrines of Worship

We commit the sin of idolatry when we try to put other things—whether activities, people, ideals, money, or anything else—above God. But why would we do that? Because we lose sight of how precious God is, how important He is, and how desperately we need Him.

✎ Read Exodus 20:4–6. What did God command His people not to do?

_____

_____

With His people surrounded by cultures that worshipped idols, God did not want them to confuse Him with any god made by human hands. We should direct our worship toward no image or idea created by us. As God essentially asks in Isaiah 40:25, "To whom can you compare Me?"

✎ Read Romans 1:21–23. What sin did these people commit toward God, as recorded in verse 21?

_____

_____

✎ And that sin led to what other sin in verses 22 and 23?

_____

_____

To praise God, we must know who He is and what He has done.

Doctrines of Service

✎ After Isaiah saw God's holiness, what did the prophet say in Isaiah 6:8?

_____

When we cherish the glory, beauty, majesty, and power of God, we have everything we need to reach out in service for Him. For those people who neglect their church family, ignore their community, and fail to give, serve, or show love—you can be sure that they have some misconception of God. Either they are not grateful for His love, or they do not trust Him to give them the grace to serve.

All Other Doctrine

It might be a little unfair to provide you a partial list in this case, but God's character dictates every single Christian teaching. We can teach no truth, no morals, no ethics, no *anything* that is not firmly grounded in who God is, as revealed in His Word.

Love, truth, grace, goodness, bondage, liberty—we could say that these are all *inter-definable* terms. Each term cannot be understood without understanding the meaning of the rest. They lean on each other like the stones of an old Roman arch—take one out, and the rest fall.

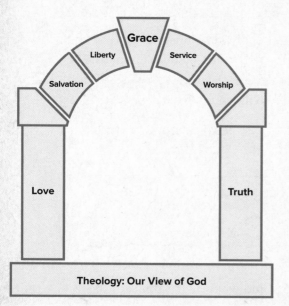

And if you change the meaning of one term, and you must change the meaning of all the rest to match. So if you find that a person has a different conception of *love* and *liberty* than you do, that person likely holds to a different definition of *truth* and *bondage*, as well.

Where then should we build our understanding of these terms? Again—on the character of God, as seen in His Word. As we see God's love and truth explained and demonstrated throughout Scripture, we can understand what He means by grace and goodness. And as we see the evil and sin shown in those same passages, we understand what it means to be in bondage—and what it means, by God's grace, to be free.

God in Both Spirit and Flesh

✎ John 4:19–24 describes God as a spirit. And how does Colossians 1:15 describe Jesus Christ?

_____

_____

✎ As God Himself, Jesus became God in the flesh. Even after His resurrection, He had a glorified body that was still physical. How do we see this physicality in Luke 24:38–43, particularly in verses 39 and 43?

_____

_____

_____

_____

✎ Yet before He ascended to heaven, Christ also demonstrated supernatural abilities that we might associate with a spirit. What was He able to do in Luke 24:30–31, 36–37?

_____

_____

_____

Application

✎ According to John 4:19–24, how is God to be worshipped?

_____

Worshipping in the Spirit

As discussed in the teacher's lesson, Christ contrasted this kind of worship with the outward, ritualistic worship performed at the Temple. To worship in the spirit is to praise God with our inner being—to fellowship with Him at the very core of our being, the part of us that, thanks to God's image, transcends our flesh and bone.

✎ According to 1 Corinthians 6:19–20, for what reason should we not commit sins against our bodies? Note also 2 Corinthians 6:16.

_____

_____

Our spirit resonates with God's. Since He dwells with us, we fellowship with Him directly—not through intermediaries or angels, as most believers did in the Old Testament. We need not perform rituals or sacrifices to symbolize God's work to come. Rather, we gather together to celebrate the work He's *already* accomplished through Christ.

✎ Read the part of Stephen's testimony in Acts 7:47–50, noting also Acts 17:24–28. According to these passages, where does God *not* need to live?

_____

_____

✎ Where instead can we fellowship with Him?

_____

_____

His Spirit is everywhere, and we can worship Him anywhere He is.

Worshipping in the Truth

Read Christ's prayer to the Father in John 17:17–19.

✎ In this passage, what did Jesus ask the Father to do for His children?

_____

✎ According to this passage, what is truth? _____

✎ What did John call Jesus, the Son of God, at the beginning of John 1:14?

_____

Truth is rooted in the person and character of God. We only know truth to the extent that we know God. Christ came to Earth in part so that we could know God and be sanctified—made holy—by His truth.

For us to worship in the truth, therefore, God must work in our hearts. As we discussed in Chapter 1, we must *know* in order to *be* in order to *do*.

We Know the Truth

We must study and rehearse the truth we find in God's Word, and we must explore His truth in all other areas of life.

We Feel the Truth

As God grows His truth in our hearts—the core of our being—we will be grateful to Him, and we will be inspired to share that truth with others. He will transform our feelings and emotions, not to a bubbly, showy kind of happiness, but to a deep, abiding joy that remains positive and hopeful even through life's harshest trials. We cannot force or fake this kind of feeling—only He can build it up over time.

We Live the Truth

Knowledge changes us, and God's knowledge changes us to be more like Him. We must reflect God's light in the way we think and act, which makes our lives a form of worship to God. Through us, people see a testimony of God's love and truth.

We Say the Truth

In the narrowest sense, however, we worship when we actively, intentionally praise God. As the angels declare God's glory in heaven, we can declare Him here on Earth—in song and praise with fellow believers, and in witness to nonbelievers.

. . . .

Notes from the Teacher's Lesson

God's Essence and Attributes

- Define *essence*: _____
  _____
  _____
  _____

- Define *attributes*: _____
  _____
  _____

God Is a Spirit

The Attributes of His Spirit

- God is _____ (Col. 1:15; John 1:18).

- God has no _____
  (Luke 24:39; Col. 1:15).

- God is in all _____ (Ps. 139:7–8).

The Significance of God's Essence as a Spirit

- We cannot know God by our _____.

- We must worship Him in _____ (John 4:24).

  ○ Through singing

  ○ Through prayer

  ○ Through service

God Is a Person

- The attributes of His personhood:

  ○ He has _____ (Isa. 55:8–9).

  ○ He has a personal _____
    which includes love (John 3:16).

  ○ He has a _____ that guides His actions (Ps. 115:3).

- The significance of His personhood (Matt. 7:9–11; Rom. 8:32):

  We define our faith as a _____.

Application Activities

1. Read and meditate on Psalm 104. Do not just record all of the things you learn of God in this passage—meditate on them, as well, and consider praying them back to the Father. Thank Him for what He is like, and apply to your life the things you learn about Him.

2. Read about—and meditate on—the way God related to Abraham in Genesis 12:10–20. This would fall under the "Biblical" category on your providence sheet.

3. For each of the following types of worship, find at least two passages of Scripture that teach us how we can pursue the activity in spirit and truth.

    A. Prayer
    B. Praise and Singing
    C. Bible Study
    D. Sharing the Gospel
    E. Practical Service—such as community outreach and philanthropy

4. Study the account of the sacrifices made by Cain and Abel in Genesis 4. In at least three paragraphs, explain why Abel's sacrifice was acceptable to God, whereas Cain's was not. What can we learn from this story today, in the age of Christ's grace?

CHAPTER 9
God's Unity

"If there be but one God, then there is but One whom you need chiefly to study to please, and that is God."

—Thomas Watson, *A Body of Divinity*

Debra was looking forward to her wedding with Allen, a smartly dressed businessman who had swept into her small English town a few months earlier. He was always moving, skipping in and out of town for meetings, yet she felt as though she knew him deeply. Everything about him seemed so driven, exciting, and purposeful.

Perhaps that's why he popped the question so quickly. Caught there in the moment, in that spot on the dry stone hedge where they loved to sit, she couldn't help but say yes. Of course, she hadn't yet introduced him to her parents. But they had pestered her for years to get married, so she doubted that they'd be too upset when they found out.

Debra didn't suspect that *she'd* be the one surprised by news of a wedding.

She found out by accident, really. She grabbed his laptop to check the next day's weather, when she saw an email open in his browser. The email wasn't suspicious at first, but then she realized that Allen had replied to it during the time he told her that he'd be outside of WIFI or cell range.

A part of her thought she was being too nosy, but then she found another email account on the laptop, one with intimate messages from a woman she didn't know.

Furious, Debra decided to talk to this woman. Was she an old girlfriend? Was Allen trying to break up with her? Debra didn't want to ask Allen until she knew more.

It wasn't difficult to track the woman down—she ran a bakery in a town not far away. Debra pretended to be a customer, bought a loaf of bread, and talked with the woman politely. Her name was Mary, and her ring finger sported a diamond even bigger than Debra's.

Debra confronted Mary about Allen. She didn't think her anger could burn any hotter, but it soon did. It took the women less than a minute to realize that they were both engaged to the same man.

A few weeks later, after some careful digging, they discovered Allen's fifteen other fiancées—and his two wives, and his children, all scattered around the country.

Allen had falsified marriage records in several counties to pull off the scheme, so the court charged him with bigamy and other misdemeanors. But thanks to the work of his lawyer—who argued that the depression caused by Allen's first wife drove him to manipulate all of these other women—Allen received only a light sentence of community service. Some of the women, still in love with him, cheered his release. The others, however, were left to pick up what remained of their lives.

The story above is inspired by a true case—one that reflects some of the darkness of human nature. We might be tempted to look down on the ignorance or infidelity of others, but don't we often betray the love of God?

The Old Testament Scriptures often compare idolatry with marital infidelity (Jer. 3:20; Hosea 3:1). We commit spiritual adultery when we worship other, lesser gods—when we forget that all good comes from the single, unified God. Do we truly focus all of our worship on Him?

Student Work

Statements of God's Unity

🖉 Read the following verses, and fill in the blanks.

- Deuteronomy 4:39—The Lord is God both in heaven and on Earth. There is _____.

- Deuteronomy 6:4—The Lord our God is _____.

- Isaiah 44:6—I am the first and I am the last . . .
  _____.

- Isaiah 45:21—There is _____ besides God.

Very little of the rest of this book will make sense if you do not believe this teaching.

🖉 For example, there is only one first cause. Read John 1:1–4. Do you think that this passage leaves room for the belief in other creators besides God? Why or why not? _____
_____
_____

How also could more than one omnipresent being exist? Or how could there be more than one infinite being above all other beings?

If God is whom He says He is, then He is one God, and no other god can compare.

Recognizing His Unity

Why does God's unity matter on a day-to-day level? How is it important to us personally?

If One God, Then One True Faith

✏ Write Ephesians 4:4–6.

_____

_____

_____

_____

_____

_____

_____

_____

God offers us one simple way to know Him—through Christ. Believers come from many backgrounds, but they are united by one path to salvation, which takes all of us by the cross of Jesus.

✏ What did Christ teach in John 14:6?

_____

_____

_____

Does this mean that we should attack and demonize people who follow other faiths? Certainly not. We have an obligation to reach out to them in love, serving them and helping them see the light of God's truth.

And don't feel bad if people tell you that you're intolerant because you trust in the absolute truth of God. After all, we must believe *something* before we can actually be tolerant. Tolerance requires informed, respectful disagreement. Tolerance based on ignorance and apathy is no tolerance at all.

So we call out darkness and lies for what they are, but we spend most of our time reflecting God's light, trusting Him to dispel ignorance and falsehood (John 1:9–17).

If One God, Then One Focus of Love and Worship

If there were many gods, then we'd be hard-pressed to please them all. What one god would like, the other gods might dislike. Thankfully, there is only one God, and through Christ's sacrifice we are His children forever.

✒ In John 4:34, what sustained Jesus as much as food or drink?

_____

✒ And in Luke 22:42, we find Jesus in the garden agonizing over the suffering that He'd face on the cross the next day. But what did He want to see accomplished, even if it conflicted with every instinct He had to avoid pain? _____ .

Everything we do—even if it's difficult, even if it helps other people—should be done to pursue God's will. And His will, we understand, is to reveal His glory (Num. 14:21; John 17:4).

In John 21, Christ shared dinner with some of His disciples shortly before He ascended to heaven. He knew that Peter would serve as a leader in the early church, and He knew what pain this friend would suffer for His sake.

✒ Knowing that all those difficulties would come, Jesus asked Peter just one question three times (21:15–17). What was it?

_____

✒ And what action should that result in?

_____

We show the love of God by declaring His truth, and we reflect His truth by showing love to others. We simply have no time to worship pleasure (2 Tim. 3:4) or our own sinful desires (1 Tim. 6:9–10).

✒ How did Asaph express his love for God in Psalm 73:25?

_____

_____

Ask God to give you that same passion and desire.

If One God, Then One Body of Believers

✒ Read John 17:20–21. Here Christ prayed for us—that is, those who believe in Him through the word of His followers. Given what He prayed in verse 21, in what way should we Christians reflect the relationship between Jesus and the Father?

_____

_____

✐ Read Galatians 3:25–29. Because we are all one in Christ, we are all equally redeemed before the Father—no matter our background (v. 28).

- Ethnicity:
  There is no _____ nor _____.

- Social or Economic Status:
  There is no _____ nor _____.

- Sex:
  There is no _____ nor _____.

✐ Using the following passages, summarize how Acts described each of the churches that sprang up under the Spirit's ministry.

- Acts 4:32–34

  _____

  _____

  _____

  _____

  _____

- Acts 5:12–14

  _____

  _____

  _____

  _____

  _____

- Acts 8:12

  _____

  _____

  _____

  _____

- Acts 10:45

  _____

  _____

  _____

  _____

- Acts 16:13–18

_____

_____

_____

_____

- Acts 17:1–4, 12

_____

_____

_____

_____

It's impossible to overstate what a break this was from tradition—men and women of all classes and backgrounds fellowshipping together, all reflecting God's love and truth.

✎ Read James 2:1–9. Briefly summarize its teaching below.

_____

_____

_____

_____

Do not try to put up walls that Christ has already torn down. Push yourself to reach out to believers of every background and status—rich and poor, male and female, old and young, unfriendly and friendly, people like you and people unlike you. As you see how God works through many different types of people, He will enrich your knowledge of His unifying grace.

If One God, Then Our God

✎ Write Psalm 48:14 below.

_____

_____

_____

_____

God is not merely _the_ God—He is also _our_ God, and that is an amazing comfort, especially in this dry, parched, weary world (Ps. 63:1).

Notes from the Teacher's Lesson

The Definition of His Unity

- There is _____.
- God is _____.

His Unity in Scripture

- In the Old Testament

    o _____

    o _____

- In the New Testament

    o _____

    o _____

The Significance of His Unity

- We _____ one God.
- We _____ one God.
- We _____ one God.

Application Activities

1. Read Psalm 106, and record all that you see about God in that passage.

2. Record any providence—in any category—that reflects our great God, who deserves love and worship.

3. Read 1 Corinthians 3:4–11, Philippians 1:12–13, and Ephesians 5:1–13.

   • For each passage, write a single paragraph summarizing its teaching.

   • Then write one or two paragraphs explaining the foundation of our unity with other believers. What determines whether we should worship and fellowship with other people?

4. Read 1 Corinthians 12:12–31.

   • Write the names of three Christians you know to whom you have not reached out in the way that you should.

   • List one or two ways that you can show love and truth to these people in the next two weeks—and then commit yourself to doing so.

The Trinity

"It is limiting to God to confine Him within the narrow compass of our reason."

—Thomas Watson, *A Body of Divinity*

Craig had enjoyed the visit with his grandmother, but he looked forward to getting home—that is, after he made it through this flight.

He had a lengthy layover at the airport before the last leg of the trip. As he sat in the terminal near the window, watching the aircraft land and take off, he saw out of the corner his eye a man walking toward him.

"Mind if I sit here?" the man asked, sitting before Craig could say anything.

"Uh, sure."

The man wore neatly ironed khakis and a pastel-blue dress shirt. The bright clothing matched the wide, stiff smile pressed into his face.

"Hi, I'm Gideon. Do you want to live with God someday?" Gideon held up a pamphlet that seemed vaguely cult-like.

Craig knew a leading question when he heard one, but as a child of God, he felt led to share what he believed about Christ. If no one had ever explained the gospel to this man, at least he would.

So Craig talked with the man, mentioning at various points in the conversation God the Father, Jesus, and the Spirit.

Gideon seemed eager to question the Trinity. "So you believe that Jesus Christ is God, right?" he asked.

"Definitely," Craig replied. "Only God could meet God's requirement of holiness. Only God could save us."

"But you also believe that the Father is God?"

"Sure—of course."

"And do you believe that the Holy Spirit is God, too?"

"Yes, they're all equally God."

"Well then," Gideon smiled, "aren't you breaking the first of the Ten Commandments—'Thou shalt have no other gods before me'? If these three people are gods, then you have three gods!"

Craig didn't know how to respond. He sat numbly while Gideon gave him an invitation to a conference, and he was relieved when he heard his flight called up for boarding.

How would you have responded to Gideon's questions? How could you have addressed his criticism of the doctrine of the Trinity?

Student Work

Now that we've discussed the essence, personality, and unity of God, we can come to only one conclusion—there is no creature in the universe like our God. He is unique among all beings, and nothing can truly compare with Him.

✎ Write Psalm 89:6 below.

_____

_____

_____

_____

_____

✎ Read Isaiah 55:9 and fill in the blanks within the summary below:

Just like the _____ are higher than the _____,

So are God's _____ higher than our _____,

And His _____ higher than our _____.

Of all the doctrines about God, the Trinity is one of the most difficult. We should therefore approach it with care and reverence—the way an experienced climber looks at an impassable wall of rock, or the way a diver looks over the edge of an underwater trench. We can only skirt the edge of this mighty truth, but looking at its height and depth will give us a greater appreciation for the majestic God who loves us.

The Doctrine of the Trinity

We find explanations of Trinitarian doctrine in the New Testament and in the writings of Christians in the first few centuries AD. This is one of the cardinal doctrines of Christian theology, and although the specific mechanics of this doctrine cannot be understood, those who deny it outright often deny the core doctrines of the gospel.

Though a deep knowledge of the Trinity is not essential for salvation—an eight-year-old believer, for example, might not be able to explain it to you—genuine, mature believers grounded in the Scripture will unanimously affirm God as three-in-one.

The word *trinity* does not occur in the Bible, but its truth is found throughout the Word. *Trinity* was coined by an early Latin Christian writer to identify the doctrine of God as three-in-one, a teaching upheld in some of the earliest Christian creeds.

As Charles Ryrie defines it,

> There is one only and true God, but in the unity of the godhead there are three eternal and co-equal persons, the same in substance but distinct in subsistence.

Note that Ryrie uses *subsistence* to refer to "beings" or "existences" that are in some way separate.

The Problem of the Trinity

The Trinity is a divine riddle, where one makes three and three make one. It is a doctrine that cannot be true if it is proved by factors within the scope of our understanding. In short, it is true because of reasons we cannot yet grasp.

It's no surprise, therefore, that many people have opposed this doctrine over the millennia. Many false teachers still claim that this idea is a lie conjured by Satan, who wants to trick believers into committing idolatry with three gods.

The logic seems simple:

- Do you believe that the Father is God? *Yes.*
- Do you believe that Jesus is God? *Yes.*
- Do you believe that the Holy Spirit is God? *Yes.*
- Then you believe in three gods.

They might use another argument, one mentioned earlier—the word *trinity* does not occur in the Scriptures. But this is a juvenile trick at best. It's like saying that *racism* did not exist until Richard Henry Pratt first used the term in 1902. We find it appropriate to use theological shorthand to encompass truth found in the Word. Doing so doesn't make the truth it defines any less true.

Another argument challenges believers to illustrate the Trinity. Since nothing can be both three and one, we can find no *perfect* illustration. We can offer close facsimiles—like St. Patrick's fabled use of a three-leaf clover—but none of these reflects the mystery exactly. God is unique, and no one should trick you into trying to prove the Trinity with metaphors or examples. If something else in the universe could perfectly reflect God, He wouldn't be the exalted, pre-eminent one.

✎ To what could we possibly compare God? Write Isaiah 40:18 below:

_____

_____

_____

_____

We can build no true image of God, either literally or metaphorically.

Statements of the Trinity

Actually, the word *trinity* might not be the best word to describe this doctrine. Why? Because it implies only half the teaching. To appreciate the Trinity, we must understand that God is unified as one, yet distinct as three. Perhaps "tri-unity" would better encompass these truths.

Old Testament Indications of Tri-Unity

✎ As discussed in the teacher's lesson, the Old Testament emphasizes the unity of the Trinity. How does each of the following verses express God's unity or oneness?

- Exodus 20:3

  _____

  _____

- Deuteronomy 4:35

  _____

  _____

- Deuteronomy 6:4

  _____

  _____

- Isaiah 45:14

  _____

  _____

- Isaiah 46:9

  _____

  _____

But the Old Testament also leaves room for a plurality to exist in this one God.

By the Use of the Word *Elohim*

Elohim is the plural form of the Hebrew word *Eloah*, meaning "God." Note its use in the following verse.

Read Deuteronomy 6:4. In the Hebrew, the structure of the verse reads as follows:

Hebrew Transliteration	*shama`*	*Yisra'el*	*Yĕhovah*	*'Elohiym*	*Yĕhovah*	*'echad*
English	Hear	Israel	Jehovah (the Lord)	God	Jehovah	is one

As discussed in the teacher's lesson, *Elohim* is a *majestic plural*, meaning it honors the subject by ascribing a figurative multiplicity to one Being. Ancient Jewish scholars did not read *Elohim* and automatically understand the doctrine of the Trinity. However, with the knowledge we have now, we can appreciate why God referred to Himself in this way.

After all, this verse is not the only place where we find the name *Elohim*. In fact, after the name *Yahweh*, *Elohim* is God's most common name in the Old Testament, with more than 2,500 uses.

By the Use of the Plural Pronouns *Us* and *Our*

For each of the following verses, write the phrase that demonstrates a plurality within God's Being.

✎ Genesis 1:26

_____

_____

✎ Genesis 11:7

_____

_____

✎ Isaiah 6:8

_____

_____

Again, God did not reveal the doctrine of the Trinity until much later, but the appearance of Christ and the Holy Spirit can now inform our reading of Old Testament Scripture.

New Testament Statements of Tri-Unity

With the revelation of Jesus and the Holy Spirit, the New Testament presents God not only as one but also as three-in-one.

Complete the following table by stating how each Person of the Trinity was involved in the events listed.

New Testament Events That Illustrate the Trinity

The Incarnation of Christ (Luke 1:35)

Father	Son	Holy Spirit

The Baptism of Christ (Matt. 3:16–17)

Father	Son	Holy Spirit

The Atonement (Heb. 9:14)

Father	Son	Holy Spirit

The Salvation of Believers (1 Pet. 1:1–2)

Father	Son	Holy Spirit

The Great Commission (Matt. 28:19)

Applications of the Doctrine

We can see at least three personal applications of the doctrine of the Trinity.

It Calls for Faith

As discussed in the teacher's lesson, the Trinity isn't something we can fully grasp. As described in the Bible, God's nature expands beyond our capacity to understand. When theologians attempt to compare the Trinity to physical objects, or when they try to systematize it or bend it to fit their logic, they often reduce its truth to something less than the Scriptures state.

But the inner workings and outer expressions of the Trinity need not make sense to us. As discussed in Chapter 1, we approach God in faith, knowing that some aspects of His essence will remain beyond our knowledge until we see Him face-to-face.

It Calls for Equal Reverence

No Person of the Godhead—the Trinity—is any more or less God than the others. The Father is not more holy, powerful, or loving than the Son or the Holy Spirit. No single Person has supereminence over another.

✎ What does John 5:23 say about this issue?

_____

_____

_____

_____

_____

_____

It Calls for Equal Obedience

The statements, commandments, and work of all three Persons are equal. The entire Trinity deserves obedience, because the entire Trinity is one God—our God.

Notes from the Teacher's Lesson

The Doctrine of the Trinity Defined

_____

_____

_____

_____

The Trinity Stated

- In the Old Testament

    ◦ Genesis 1:26

    ◦ Isaiah 6:8

- In the New Testament

    ◦ The _____ who is God (Rom. 1:7)

    ◦ The _____ who is God (Heb. 1:8;
    also Titus 2:13; John 1:3; 8:58; 10:30)

    ◦ The _____ who is God
    (Acts 5:3–4; also 1 Cor. 3:16; 2 Cor. 3:17–18)

    ◦ The Trinity presented together

        - The Great Commission (Matt. 28:19–20)

        - Paul's blessing to the Corinthians (2 Cor. 13:14)

        - Paul's explanation of the gospel to the Ephesians
        (Eph. 2:13–18)

        - Peter's blessing to believers (1 Pet. 1:1–2)

The Significance of the Trinity

- To _____ the gospel (1 Pet. 1:1–2)

- To _____ the gospel (Acts 4:12)

- To _____ (1 John 2:1; Rom. 8:26)

Application Activities

1. Consider some of the providences you've seen in your own life during the past five years. Write a brief explanation of at least three examples of providence, along with how you believe God may have used each situation for your good and His glory. If you're not yet sure, say so.

2. Using an encyclopedia or other reputable source, explain which aspects of the Trinity are denied by each of the following religions and philosophies. Briefly describe points of reasoning that contradict the teaching of the New Testament. Cite each source you use.

   A. Islam – Note Qur'an 5.72–80 (Surat Al-Ma'idah).

   B. Judaism

   C. Socinianism – sixteenth century, Poland

   D. Arianism – fourth century, Alexandria

   Note: your teacher might help you identify reputable sources.

3. List three passages from Scripture that describe the Holy Spirit making believers more holy. In your own words, briefly explain the teaching of each passage.

4. We know from Isaiah 55:8–9 that God's ways are higher than our own. His wisdom transcends and even contradicts our own. Look up the passages below, and write a brief summary of each, explaining how God's wisdom contrasts with our natural way of thinking.

   A. Proverbs 15:33

   B. Proverbs 28:13

   C. Matthew 5:44

   D. Matthew 16:25

   E. Matthew 23:11

UNIT 3
The Attributes of God

"God's glory lies chiefly in His attributes, which are the several beams by which the divine nature shines forth."

—Thomas Watson, *A Body of Divinity*

CHAPTER 11

His Omniscience

"If God be infinitely wise, let us go to Him for wisdom, as Solomon did."
—Thomas Watson, *A Body of Divinity*

You may have noticed in Scripture that when God asks a question, He already has an answer in mind. He does not ask people questions because He seeks knowledge, but because He wants people to appreciate the truth He already knows.

- "Where are you?" He asked Adam, because the first man and woman no longer walked with God (Gen. 3:9–13).

- "Where is your brother?" He asked Cain, because the first son had murdered the second (Gen. 4:9).

- "What's that in your hand?" He asked Moses, because the exiled prince wanted a sign to show his people. God could use anyone and anything to glorify Him (Exo. 4:1–2).

- "Have you considered my servant Job?" He asked Satan, because He intended to reveal His grace through the life of a faithful person (Job 1:8).

- "Where should we buy bread, so these people can eat?" He asked His disciple Philip, because He would show the multitude His power to care for them (John 6:5–6).

- "Do you love me?" He asked Peter, because the disciple needed to wrestle with the answer before he served God's children as a teacher and servant-leader (John 21:15).

When God brings a question to your mind, consider carefully its answer. Our curiosity and wonder can help us appreciate, however imperfectly, the perfect mind of God.

We call God's perfect knowledge *omniscience*—that is, His all-knowing. That attribute is the topic of this lesson.

In the previous unit, we discussed the nature of God by describing several facets of His *essence*. Now we'll begin studying His attributes, or characteristics. The teacher's lesson divides these attributes into two categories to aid your understanding:

- *Natural attributes*—which describe God's sovereign character; the qualities that help us understand His power and the scope of His rule

- *Moral attributes*—which describe how God chooses to exercise His power, particularly within His relationship to humanity

Student Work

As discussed in the teacher's lesson, God is *omniscient* in that He knows—and has always known and will always know—everything. His knowledge does not increase or decrease. He is never surprised, nor does He wonder *if*, *what*, *how*, or *why*. All truth is always known to Him because all truth flows from Him. He lives timelessly in perfect awareness of everything that was, is, and will be.

God is so far above us that sometimes it's easier to understand Him by discussing what He's *not* like. So Scripture occasionally uses a negative approach.

✎ Note, for example, Isaiah 40:13–14. How do these verses express God's perfect knowledge?

_____

_____

_____

_____

_____

The answer to those questions, of course, is *no one*. God would not be God if He needed to learn from someone else.

Omniscience Illustrated

The Bible abounds with stories and events in which we see God's omniscience. Note the following examples.

In Creation

🖉 According to Psalm 104:24, what quality did God display by making all things?

_____

As Thomas Watson wrote,

> None but a wise God could so curiously contrive the world.
>
> . . . [We can see the] wisdom of God blazing in the sun, twinkling in the stars . . . in marshalling and ordering everything in its proper place and sphere. If the sun had been set lower, it would have burnt us; if higher, it would not have warmed us with its beams. God's wisdom is seen in appointing the seasons of the year.

🖉 What does Psalm 74:17 say that God established?

_____

_____

_____

God, in His infinite wisdom, designed the wonder and complexity of the universe to showcase His glory—to fill us with wonder over His work. As we live in the rhythm of night and day, cool and warm, in the cycle of tides and seasons and harvest, we can appreciate the God who gave us not only the consistency to survive and thrive, but also the diversity to keep us surprised and delighted.

Despite the corruption from the Fall, this universe is still a precious gift marked by the wisdom and love of our Creator.

In Redemption

In God's plan of redemption we see a masterstroke that only He could have planned. God is a God of mercy and grace, yet also a God of righteousness and judgment.

As a holy God, He could not tolerate our sin. As a just God, He demanded a penalty. So in His mercy, He chose to send Jesus to Earth—to live perfectly, to bridge God and humanity, and to pay the price for our sin.

Theologians still have trouble mapping out the interaction between God's righteousness, love, and power. Yet at the cross and the tomb we see all three working in perfect harmony—God sacrificing Himself in love for us, fulfilling His own righteous requirement, defeating death and sin through His power. There we see God's great majesty beaming through even the worst of humanity.

As Watson writes,

> What wisdom was this, that Christ should be made sin, yet know no sin; that God should condemn sin, yet save the sinner! Here is wisdom, *to find out the way of salvation.*

In His Providence

"Every providence," Watson declares, "has a mercy or a wonder wrapped up in it." We see the providential wisdom of God in the following ways.

By Using Small Things

God chose to heal the snake-bitten Israelites with a simple glance at a bronze snake on a pole. He used a small stone—and a brave shepherd boy—to bring down Goliath. He used a few torches and pitchers to rout the army of the Midianites. It seems to be His habit to use what might seem small and insignificant to us.

By Doing the Opposite of What We Might Do

Which of us would have saved Jacob's family the way God did through Joseph? God advanced his servant by allowing him to be . . .

- Thrown into a pit
- Sold to slave traders
- Accused falsely of sexual assault
- Thrown into prison
- Forgotten and neglected by those he helped

Yet through these experiences Joseph became second-in-command to Pharaoh, and God in His wisdom preserved the founding family of His people, Israel.

Another illustration would be the organization of Gideon's army. When God chose to save His people from the oppression of the Midianites, how did He accomplish that end? He *decreased* the size of Gideon's army. He repeatedly told Gideon that the soldiers with him were too many (Judg. 7:2), reducing the force from a sizable 32,000 to a mere band of 300. Through this unusual move, God made sure that no one would question His hand in Israel's victory.

By Turning Evil Acts Toward Good Ends

A skilled chemist can combine several individually harmful ingredients into a single, helpful medicine. Likewise, God can orchestrate the sin and wickedness of people toward a good and worthy end.

✐ Paul recognized this truth in 2 Corinthians 4:17. How did he view the afflictions he faced?

_____

_____

_____

_____

✐ Joseph expresses this truth in Genesis 50:20, as well.

- Joseph's brothers had intended _____ against him.

- But God meant it for _____ .

In His Prophecies

✎ We see God's omniscience most clearly perhaps in His knowledge of future events. What prophecies did God reveal in the following passages?

- Genesis 15:13

  _____
  _____

- Isaiah 7:14; Micah 5:2

  _____
  _____

- Jeremiah 29:10; 2 Chronicles 36:14–21

  _____
  _____

Omniscience Applied

How should we respond to this great doctrine? We could explore many implications, but in this lesson we'll consider four brief applications.

It Illumines His Love for Us

We can rejoice and delight in God's love even more when we appreciate His omniscience.

He Knows the Worst About Us—but Still Saved Us

✎ God does not love us because we've somehow fooled Him into thinking that we're perfect people. Read Psalm 103:13–14. What does God know about us?

  _____
  _____
  _____

He knows how fleeting and pathetic we are, compared to Him, yet He still reaches out in compassion, like a loving Father.

In human relationships, we often fear that a secret about us might come to light and then break up the relationship. So we try to put on our best face with others, hiding our insecurities and not allowing ourselves to be vulnerable, even with good, safe people.

But God already knows the worst about us—and He still He saved us! He knows the wrong we have done, the wrong we might be doing now, and every wrong we will do. Yet He still promises to keep us safe in His hands, now and forever (John 10:28–29; Rom. 8:38–39).

He Sees Our Service, Even When Others Do Not

At times, the people around us don't notice the ways we try to reflect God's love and truth. They offer us no thanks or appreciation, and no one seems to care. At other times, they might even misjudge our actions, criticizing us for something we didn't do or didn't intend. They might call us failures or assume the worst motivations for our effort. Some people simply will never accept us or approve of our work. They're negative, critical people, and nothing we say or do can change their opinion. What then?

We can find comfort in the knowledge that God, who sees all things, also sees our heart. He knows our weakness and brokenness, and He knows our sin, but He still chooses to use us. Further, He glorifies Himself *through* our weakness. He sees us when we try, and He knows when we struggle to serve others in His name. We don't need to serve the fickle approval of others. Our Master is God, and no other.

He Knows What He Is Going to Make of Us

God has a purpose for each of us, a purpose so important that He sent Christ to die for us. God redeemed us to glorify Himself—to become more holy, to be more like Him.

✏ Read Romans 8:28–29. To what did God predestine us?

_____

_____

God will bring us to this end. Although we fall and fail, sin and slip, God still works—even through our failures—to make us like Himself.

Don't lose sight of Him. Don't stop seeking the One who will one day present us before His throne as blameless, spotless, and pure.

It Comforts Us in Difficulties

✎ How did God's omniscience comfort Job, even in the middle of his trials (Job 23:10)?

_____

_____

_____

_____

God knows every trial, tribulation, sorrow, and heartache. Though we cannot yet understand why, He allows these to occur in some way for our good and His glory.

It Encourages Us to Rely on Him for Wisdom

God knows the bad way, the good way, the better way, and the best way. He knows the trials and pitfalls along each path, and He offers us His wisdom. We have only to ask for it (James 1:5). His Word and His Spirit provide us a guide through the winding maze of life.

To refuse His wisdom seems like folly. But how many times do we make decisions without consulting Him? When God inspired His Word, He knew every detail of every moment of our lives. We can rest assured that its truth applies to us.

It Discourages Us from Betraying Him

Few things sober people more than the thought of being caught in sin by someone they love. Meditate on this for a moment. The God who loves us—the God who endured a life and a death of suffering and shame for us, the God who gave us every good thing in our lives—watches over us. To sin against Him and against others is to betray His love and care.

✎ This should dominate our thoughts when we face temptation. Read Psalm 139:11–12. What two things are alike to God?

_____

_____

God holds us accountable for our actions, regardless of who else sees them.

After Sarah beat her servant Hagar and drove her into the wilderness, the "Angel of the Lord"—which was God Himself—appeared to Hagar. The Angel comforted her, assuring her that after she left Abraham's family for good, God would preserve her and her son Ishmael, whose descendants would form a mighty nation.

Hagar was so overwhelmed at this unexpected appearance that she exclaimed "*La Hai Roi*"—that is, "God sees me." In Genesis 16:14, we read that she named the well in that spot *Beer-lahai-roi* as a memorial that God sees all, even those abused and rejected by others.

We can be comforted and sobered by God's omniscience. It should affect not only our actions and speech, but also our thoughts and motives. Every secret evil is as plain to Him as the most boisterous good deed.

Celebrate God's perfect, knowing love, and let it challenge you to better reflect Him to others.

Notes from the Teacher's Lesson

The Attributes of God

Natural Attributes	Moral Attributes

The Definition of Omniscience

- _____
  _____
  _____

The Statement of Omniscience

- _____

The Significance of Omniscience

- To _____ (Prov. 15:3; Ps. 10:7–11)

- To _____ (Rom. 8:28–29)

Application Activities

1. Read Psalm 139 and record all of the things you learn about God's omniscience in those verses. Note especially verses 1–6 and 14–24.

2. Consider an example of providence in your own life that, at the time it happened, you could not understand. Yet, looking back, you might begin to understand part of God's purpose. Write about the circumstances on a personal providence sheet.

3. Write a three-page overview of a Christian that God used through incredibly difficult circumstances.

   - For your source material, read a biography, or conduct research on a contemporary Christian figure who serves God despite opposition.

   - If this person is alive, consider writing him or her a note of encouragement, along with perhaps some questions to enhance your writing.

   - Cite at least three sources in your work, and document any personal research you perform.

   - Your teacher may also ask you to briefly present your paper to your classmates.

CHAPTER 12

His Omnipresence

"God's essence is not limited either to the regions above, or to the terrestrial globe, but is everywhere."

—Thomas Watson, *A Body of Divinity*

Joy was home alone. Her parents, sister, and two brothers were away for the afternoon, and the house was very quiet. Joy decided that it was a perfect time to catch up on some of her writing.

She finished compiling a few of her notes into an extra page for her short story. But just as she began to type an email to a missionary friend, she sensed a sudden strangeness in the room. The quiet house had gotten even quieter, and the silence felt eerie. Something was missing.

Gradually, Joy realized what it was. The refrigerator's motor wasn't running. The whirr of the overhead fan had died down as well, and the air conditioner no longer hummed in the background.

Joy saw the battery indicator on her laptop—the house's power had gone out.

She had become so used to the soundscape of her home, with its consistent hum and whir of appliances, that she didn't notice how loud it really was until it all went away. The silence was almost unnerving, and when she heard the wind and the crickets outside, she chuckled to herself. It had been a while since she stopped and noticed the sounds of nature.

God never leaves us, but we can get so caught up with everything else that we fail to appreciate His presence. We allow too much to distract us from our true comfort, our true joy, and our true hope.

In Genesis 28 we read the account of Jacob's dream, in which God told him that He would be with him and keep him no matter where he went. When Jacob awoke, he exclaimed, "Surely the Lord is in this place, and I knew it not!"

The Scripture teaches us that God is *everywhere* and *in everything*. We call this the doctrine of God's *omnipresence*. Few things would jar our worldview more than a full realization of this truth. It's easy to sin against a distant God—but much more difficult to betray the Friend who has stayed with you every step of the way.

During this lesson, ask God to increase your awareness of His presence, and then find ways to practice this knowledge daily. Know that He is here, and thank Him.

Student Work

Omnipresence in Scripture

✎ Read each passage carefully, and then match the reference to the phrase that best summarizes the passage's teaching on omnipresence.

1.		Some sinful people would rather die than face the judgment of God's presence.	**A.** Psalm 139:7–12
2.		Even some of God's people try to run from Him.	**B.** Jeremiah 23:23–24
3.		Other so-called gods in the Old Testament were not omnipresent.	**C.** Matthew 28:20
4.		God fills both heaven and the earth. No secret places exist beyond His presence.	**D.** 1 Kings 8:27; Isaiah 66:1
5.		Heaven and the earth cannot contain God.	**E.** 1 Kings 18:27
6.		God's presence extends beyond heaven, beyond death, and beyond the farthest reaches of the sea.	**F.** Jonah 1:3
7.		God dwells in every Christian.	**G.** 1 Corinthians 6:19
8.		Christ is always with us.	**H.** Revelation 6:15–17

✎ Read Acts 17:24–28, and write verse 24 below:

_____

_____

_____

_____

_____

✎ Even though God allowed humanity to spread out over the face of the earth, what did He expect them to do (v. 27)?

_____

✎ Note the end of verse 27. Why are people able to find God, if they seek Him?

_____

Applications of Omnipresence

An awareness of God's presence can bring . . .

- Comfort and fellowship in loneliness (Matt. 28:19–20)

- Faith in impossible situations, or when you are totally misunderstood. How might this truth have helped David in 1 Samuel 30:6?

_____

_____

_____

_____

_____

- Protection in danger (Ps. 91:9–16)

- Caution against temptation (Jer. 23:23–24)

God Knows the Heart of Every Person

✎ Summarize what each verse says that God can do in a person's heart. Two examples are completed for you.

- 1 Samuel 16:7

  _____

  _____

- 1 Kings 4:29

  _____

  _____

- Psalm 7:9
  God tests the minds and hearts of people to discern good and evil.

- Proverbs 21:1

  _____

  _____

- Isaiah 57:15

  _____

  _____

- Jeremiah 24:7

  _____

  _____

- Hebrews 4:12
  The Word of God is a living Word. He uses it to discern and reveal the thoughts and intentions of the heart.

- Ephesians 3:16–19

  _____

  _____

  _____

Notes from the Teacher's Lesson

The Definition of Omnipresence

_____

_____

The Statement of Omnipresence *(Ps. 139; Jer. 23:23–24)*

Common Questions:

- Does God occupy uninhabited places (Jer. 23:24; Col. 1:17)?

  _____

  _____

- Is God in hell (2 Thess. 1:8–9)? _____

- What's the difference between omnipresence and pantheism?

  ○ Pantheism

  _____

  ○ Omnipresence

  _____

  _____

- Why did God "dwell" in the Tabernacle and Temple (1 Kings 8:27–30)?

  _____

  _____

  _____

The Significance of Omnipresence

- No one can _____
  (Ps. 139:7–12; Jer. 23:23–24; Jonah 1:3).

- God knows _____ and controls _____ (Prov. 21:1).

- God is present in every _____
  (1 Cor. 6:19; Col. 1:27).

- God knows the heart of every person (1 Sam. 16:7).

Application Activities

1. Read Psalm 139 and record all of the things that you learn about God's omnipresence.

   - In how many different places did the psalmist note God's presence?

   - What lessons did he learn?

   - What are your thoughts and reflections on this psalm? Note especially verses 3, 5, 7–13, and 15–16.

2. Write three paragraphs about the presence of God.

   - How do you think we can feel or know His presence with us?

   - Cite at least two people from the Bible who took comfort specifically in God's presence.

3. Pick two religions other than Christianity, and explain how their doctrine addresses the concept of divine omnipresence—or how it does not. Write a paragraph for each religion, and then write a third paragraph comparing and contrasting their doctrine with Christian teaching on God's omnipresence. Use only reputable sources, and cite any you use. Note: your teacher might help you identify reputable sources.

4. Compose a poem or a song on the theme of God's omnipresence.

CHAPTER 13

His Omnipotence

"He can do what He will; His power is as large as His will."

—Thomas Watson, *A Body of Divinity*

Ray sat upright in bed with a start. His heart raced wildly, and he found himself gasping for air.

He had never heard a louder clap of thunder. The house had shaken, and his eyes still burned with the after-image of lightning outside his window. A severe thunderstorm must have arisen shortly after he went to bed.

Ray heard a large snap outside, and he reached his window in time to see his neighbor's tree begin to topple over in the rain. He saw smoke—did the lightning strike it? The leaves in the branches hissed as they fell toward the ground.

Ray felt moisture on the windowsill. He looked up—a small bead of water trailed down from the ceiling. Was the roof leaking? Was the wind really that strong? He grabbed a towel from the bathroom, put it on the still, and stood gazing out at the raging storm.

He loved to watch the play of lightning in the clouds. Each flash illuminated everything in the neighborhood as if it were midday. Ray saw leaves whipping off his neighbor's fallen tree. That was going to take forever to clean up.

He heard a knock at his door behind him.

"Ray?" His mother called. "We need to get downstairs—*now*. Grab your shoes and let's go."

"What's the matter, Mom?" Ray asked, getting dressed, putting on his shoes, and grabbing his phone. "Did you see the lightning strike that hit Gerry's tree?"

Ray's door slammed open. Light spilled in from the hallway, where his sisters ran past his mom toward the stairs.

"Hey, wait a sec—"

"Ray—move *now*," his mom interrupted him. "We're getting an alert. There might be a tornado in the area. I have the flashlights and the storm kit."

They huddled together in the downstairs bathroom—Ray, his mom, and his two little sisters. He'd never seen them this quiet. His mom had tried getting the two to sing, but they were cut off when another lightning strike hit nearby. Now they all kept checking the weather on their phones.

Just when Ray opened a bottle of water, the power snapped off, and the bathroom remained lit with the blue glow of his phone's screen. Then they heard a terrible roar—one much louder and longer than any they had heard before. With an awful clarity Ray understood what all those warnings had meant—*it did sound like a train.*

Before anything else crossed his mind, Ray hugged his sisters to him, just as they could hear several loud bangs and creaks upstairs. He didn't know what would happen, but he knew that he'd keep his sisters with him. Mom huddled close, and they all flinched as they heard glass shatter. What followed was an even louder roar. Ray felt a drop of pressure in his ears.

The noise subsided quickly, much to Ray's surprise. His mom got another alert—the tornado had left the area, and it was no longer touching ground.

After waiting another twenty minutes, Ray ventured out into the living room. His shoes squished in the carpet, and he saw that the picture window had completely shattered. He saw leaves and bits of other debris scattered around the entire room. Outside he could see flashes of light. Sparks leapt from the transformer near Gerry's house, and broken power lines lay tangled in fallen trees.

Later, in the light of day, they found that three houses in their town had been completely destroyed by the tornado. The news reported that three people had been killed, with a few more injured.

Ray was surprised to see that some structures had shingles or siding torn away, whereas others looked barely touched. Trees lay everywhere.

As he helped Gerry split apart his tree, Ray realized that he wanted to understand more about extreme weather—what caused it, what directed it, and how he could help people survive it. Could this be some kind of calling?

"Remember that awe you feel now," his mother told him, helping him lift a larger branch. "As much as we try to live sheltered and removed from nature, its power is all around us. And it's only a taste of what God controls."

· ·

Student Work

Statements of Omnipotence in Scripture

Read the following passages, and write the letter of each passage next to the statement that best summarizes its message about God's omnipotence.

1.		No one on Earth can keep God from accomplishing His will.	**A.** Revelation 19:6
2.		God is Almighty, and He uses His power to establish covenants and promises with those who trust Him.	**B.** Isaiah 46:10–11
3.		God's power does not tire or weaken.	**C.** Daniel 4:35; Job 42:2
4.		God will accomplish everything He has purposed, or planned, to do.	**D.** Psalm 33:6–9;
5.		God is—and will continue to be—praised in heaven for His omnipotent rule.	Jeremiah 32:17
6.		God created the heavens, the earth, and the seas by speaking.	**E.** Colossians 1:15–17
7.		God can do more than we could ever dream, and His power is at work within us.	**F.** Ephesians 3:20–21
8.		Everything was created by Christ and for Christ. By His power everything continues to hold together.	**G.** Genesis 17:1–2 **H.** Isaiah 40:28

Areas of Omnipotence

God's omnipotence manifests in many ways, including in the following major areas.

Over Creation

In His Act of Creation

✎ Read Psalm 33:6–9 again. According to verse 9, how did God create the world? _____

✎ According to Hebrews 11:3, what did God use to create the universe we see? _____

From these verses, many theologians infer that God created the universe *ex nihilo*—that is, from nothing. Under this view, the "waters" described in Genesis 1:2 represented a matterless void.

Clearly, God needs no instrument or material with which to work, though He did form humanity using the dust, or base elements, of the ground (Gen. 2:7).

In His Control of Nature

The complex power of nature is itself an example of God's might. But He has also chosen to show His omnipotence by checking nature's power. His Creation has not broken free of His grasp.

✎ Read each of the following passages, and describe how God showed His control over nature.

• Psalm 107:23–29

_____

_____

_____

• Daniel 3:19–25

_____

_____

_____

- Isaiah 38:8

  _____
  _____
  _____
  _____

- Daniel 6:22

  _____
  _____
  _____

Over Angels

✎ God has sometimes sent angels to accomplish His will. Which passages in the previous list showed angels exercising their power in service to God? _____

✎ List at least two other examples of God demonstrating His power through the work of angels. Include Scripture references for both.

  _____
  _____
  _____
  _____
  _____

✎ And whom has God commanded angels to help now (Heb. 1:14)?

  _____

Over Humanity

✎ Read Daniel 4:35 and write its meaning in your own words.

  _____
  _____
  _____
  _____
  _____
  _____

Over Satan

✎ How is God's power over Satan shown in the following verses?

- Job 1:12; 2:6

  _____

  _____

- Matthew 4:1–11

  _____

  _____

  _____

- Revelation 20:7–10

  _____

  _____

  _____

  _____

Over History

While the meaning behind much of the Bible's prophetic books (e.g., Ezekiel, Daniel, Revelation) is still vague, their primary message is clear—God controls history, and He will drive it toward the moment when all of heaven and Earth will reflect His perfect light. We need not fear when we see clouds gather or hear war cries grow loud. Our God is the omnipotent Ruler of all nations.

Over Sin

The same power that drew Christ from the grave also draws us from sin to salvation. The same power that formed us now redeems us from corruption.

In the ministry of Christ we find many miracles—He made the blind to see, He made the deaf to hear, and He even raised the dead back to life. While these miracles revealed the compassion of Christ, they also served a greater purpose.

✎ Read Mark 2:1–12. What did Jesus ask the scribes in verse 9?

_____

_____

_____

_____

✎ Why did Jesus heal this man publicly (vv. 10–11)?

_____

_____

_____

Applications of Omnipotence

What do we do with this knowledge? Read the following passages, and state in your own words what each example of power should mean to you.

- Psalm 33:6–8

  _____

  _____

- 1 Peter 1:3–5

  _____

  _____

- 2 Corinthians 9:8 and 1 Thessalonians 5:24

  _____

  _____

  _____

  _____

- Genesis 50:20; Romans 8:28

  _____

  _____

  _____

  _____

God's power can awe and inspire us, but we must not forget that His might is shaped and directed by His love. God Almighty is a benevolent God who works everything for the good of those who trust Him.

Notes from the Teacher's Lesson

The Definition of Omnipotence

- Defined positively:

  _____

  _____

- Defined negatively:

  God does not contradict or oppose Himself.

  ○ He is the God of truth, so He does not lie (Heb. 6:18).

  ○ He is the holy God, so He does not accept evil in His presence (Hab. 1:13).

  ○ He is the mighty God, so evil cannot truly tempt Him (James 1:13).

  ○ He is the faithful and loving God, so He does not disown His children, in whom His Spirit dwells (2 Tim. 2:13).

The Statement of Omnipotence

  _____

The Significance of Omnipotence

- We can have peace despite _____
  (John 19:8–11).

- We can have peace despite _____
  (Prov. 16:7).

- We represent God's _____ (Phil. 4:13).
  We can do all things through Christ, who gives us strength. When God calls us to do something for Him, He will enable us to do it.

Application Activities

1. Read Psalm 33 and list all of the things you see about God in this passage. Pray the passage back to God, and take time to meditate on God's power, thanking Him for His work in your life.

2. Meditate on the providence of God shown in the Book of Daniel. Pick any narrative from the book, and complete a providence journal entry using that passage.

3. Conduct a study of the name *El Shaddai*, which is one of the names of God. In three paragraphs, describe the meaning of the name while citing a few examples of its use in the Bible.

4. Read Psalm 107:23–43.

   • List three things from nature that awe or inspire you. Using your science textbook or another reputable source, describe each example in one paragraph. Note: your teacher might help you identify reputable sources.

   • Explain in a fourth paragraph why many people look at these same things and attribute none of this glory to God.

CHAPTER 14

His Eternality

"Study God's eternity; it will make us adore where we cannot fathom."

—Thomas Watson, *A Body of Divinity*

Light travels at the phenomenal speed of 299,792 kilometers per second. One light-year—that is, the distance light will travel in one year—is roughly 9.4605×10^{12} km. That's over nine trillion kilometers.

By this measurement, the closest star to our sun, Alpha Centauri, is 4.367 light-years away. Arcturus lies more than 36 light-years away, while Spica is over 260 away. The star Deneb is the brightest in the constellation Cygnus, and one of the most remote we can see with the naked eye. Estimates place Deneb's distance between 1,400 and 3,200 light-years away. Yet as a white-hot supergiant, this star remains among the brightest in our sky.

Those four stars move within our galaxy, the Milky Way, which scientists estimate to be 100,000 light-years wide. In this vast whirlpool of stars, our solar system lies about 26,000 light-years from the galactic center.

Beyond our galaxy we can see others—more than fifty in our Local Group, including the Andromeda Galaxy, which is around 2.5 million light-years from us. And still more lie beyond—with the galaxy EGS8p7 perhaps even 13 billion light-years away.

Among the farthest reaches are quasi-stellar objects—*quasars* for short. Like many distant objects, quasars are receding from us so fast that their light reaches us *redshifted*. Some quasars may be traveling up to 90% the speed of light, which means that the light they send toward us stretches into longer wavelengths toward the red end of the visible spectrum—and even deeper, into infrared or radio waves. Astronomers believe that quasars might be supermassive black holes surrounded by the beginnings of a galaxy or the remnants of one. Either way, these objects must emit unimaginable amounts of energy to reach us—perhaps even the light of a trillion stars.

And within this vast universe hides incredible mysteries. At the beginning of the twenty-first century, scientists rely on the Standard Model, a theory of particle physics that successfully describes and predicts the behavior of matter, as governed by four key forces—electromagnetism, gravity, weak nuclear, and strong nuclear. This model builds on quantum field theory, which presents the universe as a system of interconnected fields—one field for each kind of particle. Individual particles—like electrons and photons—are therefore excited little bits of energy that move along their own fields. These fields somehow interact at the particle level to form what we call atoms. Of course, no one picture or description can adequately describe the forces at work, but mathematical models help us understand more.

However, the Standard Model does not yet account for so-called *dark matter and energy*. Since dark matter does not interact with electromagnetism, it does not emit or absorb light. In fact, light seems to pass right through it, even though dark matter's apparent gravity is stronger than that of visible matter by six or seven times. So while scientists can measure dark matter's gravitational effect on the visible universe, they cannot yet see it or describe what it *is*.

And this isn't the quirk of some small handful of material. According to current estimates, dark matter and energy make up the vast majority of our universe, leaving scientists with a model that—while very robust—explains only the visible 5%.

Our universe is very, very big, and the vast majority of it operates on levels we do not fully understand. Therefore, when God says that He is eternal and transcendent, it is no small claim. The god of a shrine or a tribe need not be very big, but our God claims ownership of the Earth, the Moon, the Sun, and all the other stars. And He does not merely own the heavens—He designed and made them.

Even a simple look up at the stars can lead us, like David, to ask God, "What then are we, that You are mindful of us?" (Ps. 8:3–4).

Student Work

Applications of God's Eternality

As we choose to meditate on God's eternality, we can appreciate the following truths.

God Is Knowable and Predictable

You may have heard people say, "That's not the person I knew before." A husband or a wife might grow distant from a spouse. Someone might discover a shocking revelation about a friend. A graduate might see fellow students at a reunion, but recognize only a few of them.

God is not like that. He never changes. If He seems different to you now than He was five years ago, it is because your knowledge of Him has grown or because you have forgotten parts of His character.

Therefore, it is important to study how God interacted with humanity throughout history. God did not change between the Old and New Testaments, even if the latter revealed more of His plan.

✎ Read 1 Corinthians 10:1–11, which describes God's relationship with Israel during their wandering in the wilderness. According to verses 6 and 11, why did the Scriptures record these events for us?

_____

_____

_____

_____

_____

Even though we live in the age of grace, we can learn from the way God dealt with His people in ancient times. If the focus of our study is God, then the focus of our study will not change, regardless of what passage we read.

God Redeemed Us for Eternity

✎ God will never change His mind about our salvation. Salvation does not depend on how we act, but on what He did, so we can rest assured that we are redeemed eternally. How did Christ picture this safety in John 10:28–29?

_____

_____

God is greater than all. He preceded all, so no one and nothing can surprise Him now.

We Have an Eternal Outlook

Because God is eternal, and His life is ours, we, too, are eternal creatures. We can see past this world into the eternity beyond, so we should make decisions and value judgments from this privileged perspective.

✎ Hebrews 11:24–26 describes the outlook of Moses. What did he give up, and what did he pursue?

_____

_____

_____

_____

_____

✎ Read Matthew 6:19–21. What did Christ say happens to treasure we store up on Earth?

_____

_____

_____

These passages apply to more areas than money or material treasure. They teach us what should occupy our attention, time, and energy. What will matter in eternity—what goals, what purposes, what change?

Our heart will rest with our treasure. We can be uplifted or destroyed by what we value. Be careful, therefore, where you point your desire and affection.

In the following table, list some things that will not count for eternity—and some that *will*. Give four examples from each category.

Temporarily Significant	Eternally Significant

What rules your thoughts—temporal values or eternal ones? What matters to you? What do your time, energy, hopes, and desires say about what you value? Do you fill your life with so many hobbies and activities that you have no time to pray, study the Word, or share God's truth with others?

God has given us a wonderful world to explore now—and we certainly should—but we should know that this is only a temporary, corrupted home. Our true resting place is with the God of eternity.

Notes from the Teacher's Lesson

The Definition of Eternality

- _____
  _____

- Three types of beings:
  - Those that have a beginning and an end: _____
  - Those who have a beginning, but no end:
    _____
  - One Being who has no beginning and no end: _____

The Statement of Eternality

- _____

The Significance of Eternality

- God's _____ extends forever
  (Rev. 20:9–15).

- God's _____ extend forever
  (1 Thess. 4:17; Rev. 21:1–5)

- We should live as _____
  would live (Eccles. 3:11).

Application Activities

1. Study the life of Hezekiah in 2 Kings 18–21, and record all of the ways that you see God work in these chapters. Write at least two principles about God that you can apply to your own life.

2. Complete a providence sheet using an example of God's work in 2 Kings 18–21.

3. Choose and read a reputable book on astronomy, noting at least five facts, ideas, or theories that expand your appreciation for God's work in our universe. Write a brief summary of each item, as well as a paragraph describing what you believe we can learn about God from the heavens. Note: your teacher might help you identify reputable sources.

4. Find a contemporary or historical astronomer who is also a Christian, and research what he or she has said about how faith affects an approach to science. Using at least two sources, summarize the astronomer's beliefs in three paragraphs.

5. Research and briefly describe three different methods that scientists use to estimate the distance between Earth and a celestial object. If you wanted to participate in such projects in the future, what disciplines should you study in high school and beyond?

6. Search online for pictures of space. Paint or draw your own picture based on what you found.

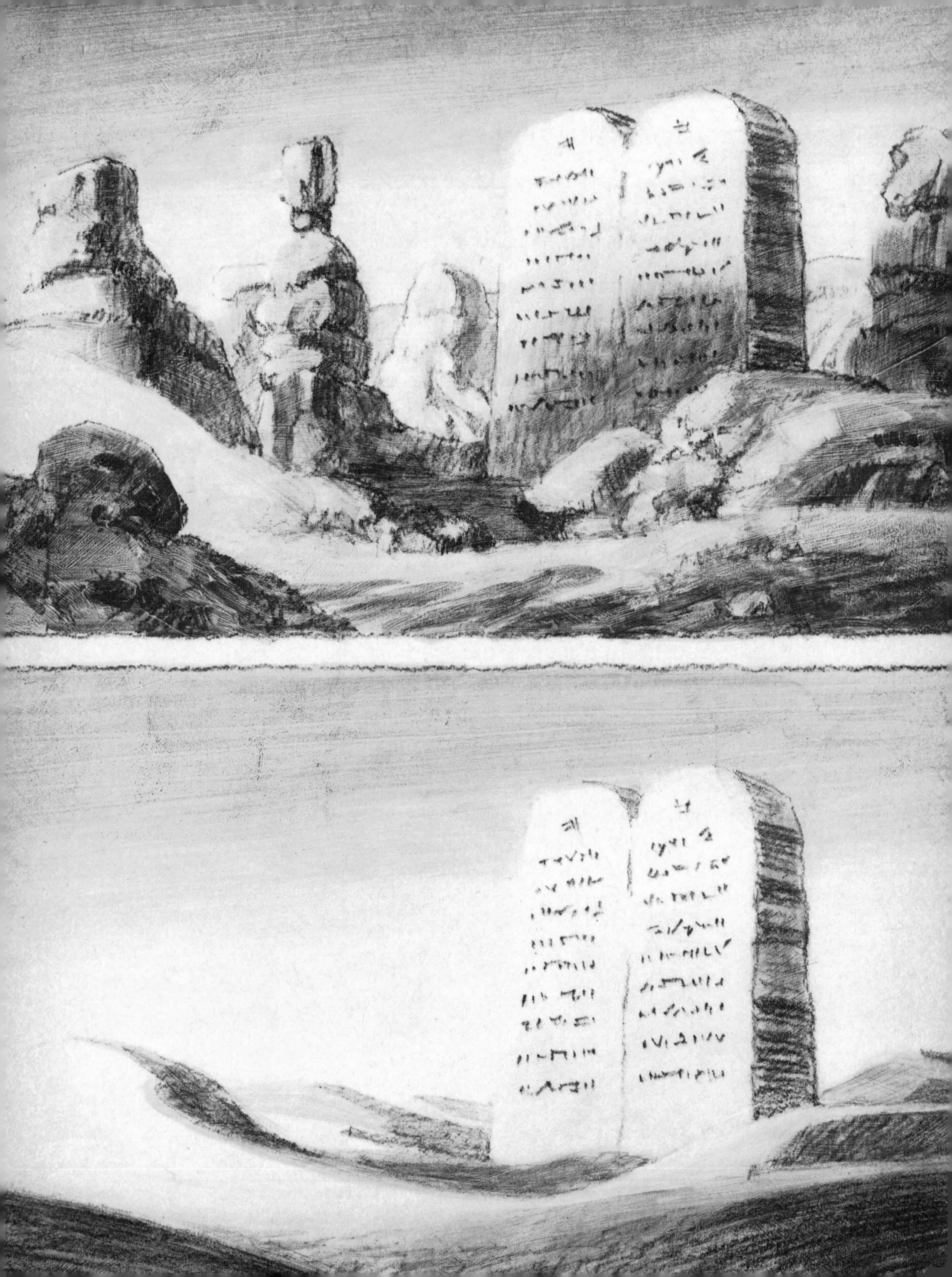

CHAPTER 15

His Immutability

"What He has decreed from eternity is unalterable. God's eternal counsel or decree is immutable."

—Thomas Watson, *A Body of Divinity*

To be human is to change. God has built inside us the incredible capacity to grow, learn, and adapt, and His Spirit continues to sanctify us as we dwell in Him. To fear change often means fearing improvement.

But not all change is good. We can, for example, go back on our word. We turn our promises into lies, and we can cover up the truth to hide our betrayal. Nearly everyone can list lies that have hurt them over their lifetime. Every history book overflows with examples of betrayal. Business contracts, political promises, international treaties—all are written with the understanding that people break their word. What do many lawyers, accountants, therapists, soldiers, police, and locksmiths have in common? They have an income because people—even people we love—cannot be trusted.

Isn't anyone completely trustworthy? Who can we take at their word? Only one—God. He is the same yesterday, today, and forever (Heb. 13:8). He does not lie (Num. 23:19; Titus 1:2), so when He says something, we can trust Him to keep His word. He is the Lord Jehovah, and He does not change (Mal. 3:6).

As we learn to trust God, we'll learn to trust those people who also rely on Him. No one is perfect, and all of us will fail, but God can help us trust people who have shown themselves to be loving and gracious.

As noted in this chapter's teacher's lesson, the doctrines of eternality and immutability are closely linked, but it is this second attribute that we will study in this lesson.

Student Work

Overview

The word *immutable* means "unchanging." God is immutable in that He does not change—He's always the same.

Eternality implies immutability. If our God stands above the constraints of time, it only makes sense that time does not change Him the way it does us. What God was a thousand years ago, He is today. He looks down on the past, the present, and the future from the same fixed vantage point. Therefore, the God who talked to Adam and Eve is the same God who communes with us.

✎ Look up every reference listed below, checking off each passage that you believe states or indicates the immutability of God.

☐ Numbers 23:19	☐ Psalm 119:89	☐ Job 23:13
☐ Psalm 33:11	☐ Ecclesiastes 7:13	☐ Proverbs 19:21
☐ Ecclesiastes 3:14	☐ Isaiah 59:1	☐ Isaiah 31:2
☐ Isaiah 40:28	☐ Romans 11:29	☐ Hosea 13:14
☐ Malachi 3:6	☐ Psalm 102:27	☐ Hebrews 6:17
☐ James 1:17	☐ 2 Corinthians 1:20	☐ Hebrews 13:8
☐ John 8:57	☐ Hebrews 7:25	☐ Isaiah 14:24

✎ Write the passage that you believe best states the immutability of God. Include the reference.

_____

_____

_____

_____

_____

_____

_____

_____

_____

Facets of God's Immutability

Let's quickly look at four things that never change about God.

God's Character Never Changes

God's love is always the same. He never loves us more at any one moment than He does at any other moment. Therefore—and this is important—*we can do nothing to make Him love us more.*

Likewise, God's hatred of sin never changes. He treats sin now just as He has always treated it. This hatred is not a reversal of God's love, but another expression of the same character. It only makes sense that goodness and light oppose evil and darkness.

If God's character changed, then He would not be God. Unlike us, He does not get better or worse. He will not ever be *more* or *less* perfectly God. He is always holy and perfect.

> **Application:** We can therefore trust His Person. We don't need to worry about Him changing or being fickle. We can always come to Him in prayer and receive the same grace each day and each moment.
>
> He will not lie about the gifts that He gives us, nor will He repent from giving them. He's seen our entire lives before we were even born, and He did not redeem us by accident. We need not walk around Him on eggshells. He is our perfect, unchanging Father, and we can rest in His arms.

God's Truth Never Changes

God's Word is eternal. He never changes His mind or rewrites His Scripture. What He says will stand eternally.

✎ According to Matthew 5:18, what did Christ say would fall away from the Law?

_____

_____

God holds His Word eternally fixed in heaven (Ps. 119:89). No matter what people try to change here on Earth, His truth will never change.

Application: We can trust God's promises. Whatever God says will happen, will happen. He will fulfill His Word because His Word is an extension of His unchanging character.

✎ Summarize in your own words the teaching of James 1:17 and 2 Corinthians 1:20.

_____

_____

_____

_____

_____

_____

God's Purpose Never Changes

Before God created the world, He devised a plan to redeem us from our sin, according to His own purpose and will (Eph. 1:11–14). He has never altered that plan, nor will He ever deviate from it. God's purpose is as timeless as He is.

Application: We can trust God's plan. We need never fear the news or the plots of other people. God is always in control, and He uses even the wickedness of humans to further His purpose.

✎ Read Psalm 33:11 and Isaiah 14:24; 46:10. According to these passages, what stands forever?

_____

God's Son Never Changes

✎ Write Hebrews 13:8 below:

_____

_____

_____

_____

This statement reaffirms the deity of Jesus Christ. He has the same attributes as the Father. Since only God can have such attributes, Christ must be God.

Application: We can trust God's salvation. Because Christ is eternally the same, we know that He is eternally sinless. Therefore, His perfect sacrifice is never at risk.

✎ In 2 Timothy 1:1, what does Paul call the life we have in Jesus Christ?

_____

_____

And God, who is unchanging, will surely keep it.

In these facets of God's immutability, we can see the following grace:

- His immutability gives us security.

- His immutability gives us comfort.

- His immutability gives us faith. We know that we have every reason to trust Him and His promises.

- His immutability gives us stability. We can plan, trust, make decisions, and rest because we learn to trust His work in our lives.

- His immutability gives us fellowship. What we learn about God today will not change tomorrow. And since God is always the same, we can bond with other Christians over our shared experience of His grace.

If our infinitely complex God changed, we could never hope to know Him. Understanding Him is difficult enough now. Change would make it impossible, like trying to decode a signal with a key that keeps evolving.

But God stands fixed, and our lives can be more stable if we build them around Him. Change and growth and movement will always be necessary here on Earth, but we can find inner peace in the eternal Giver of good gifts.

So study Him. Nothing you learn of Him will be wasted. And the more you know Him, the more you will know how to enjoy Him and reflect His unique Person.

Notes from the Teacher's Lesson

The Definition of Immutability

* _____
  _____
  _____

The Ways in Which God Is Immutable

* In His _____ (James 1:17)

* In His _____ (Isa. 40:8)

* In His _____ (Isa. 46:8–11)

* In His _____ (Heb. 13:8)

Application Activities

1. Read 1 Samuel 15, and meditate on God's immutability as shown in that passage. Write the following things from the passage:

   A. God's command to Saul

   B. Saul's response to this command

   C. The reason Saul disobeyed the command

   D. What God desired most in Saul

   E. What God thinks of rebellion and disobedience

   F. God's punishment for Saul

   G. God's unchanging character

   H. God's unchanging truth

   I. God's unchanging principles

   J. God's unchanging purpose

2. Study how David succeeded Saul as King of Israel. Complete a providence sheet using these passages, with God's immutability as your focus.

3. As we grow in the knowledge and grace of God, we will become more like our Father. Write at least two paragraphs explaining how we can reflect God's immutability our . . .

   • Character

   • Truthfulness

   • Purpose

   • Relationship to Christ

   Write a third paragraph explaining how some people might misapply immutability to their lives. In what ways *should* we change?

CHAPTER 16

His Holiness

"God is not only a pattern of holiness, but He is a principle of holiness: His spring feeds all our cisterns, He drops His holy oil of grace upon us."

—Thomas Watson, *A Body of Divinity*

To write a good love story, the old wisdom goes, you have to build a big wall. A mother has to overcome hardship and trial to care for her child. A man and a woman have to overcome their differences to understand and accept each other. We often measure love by the barriers it breaks down.

The father of the prodigal son showed incredible love and forgiveness, despite the sins of one son and the jealousy of the other. Ruth and Boaz overcame sorrow and prejudice to be together. The prophet Hosea forgave his wife despite repeated betrayal.

And God, whose love is reflected in all of the examples above, broke down the biggest wall *ever* to forgive us—the wall of our sin, which removed us from His absolute holiness. He is uniquely exalted and completely sinless, and our sin allowed us nowhere near the majesty of His presence.

But God took on Himself the body of a human, choosing to live among sinful, helpless people like us. He endured the hardships of human life, the trials of an earthly ministry, and the suffering of a cruel death. But through all of this, He remained holy for our sake, ensuring that His death would serve as the spotless sacrifice that His own justice required.

God is still absolutely holy, but through Christ we can now commune with Him, and through the Spirit we can grow more like Him, reflecting Him better each day.

To begin our study of the moral attributes of God, we will therefore study God's holiness—which, as noted earlier, is the pinnacle of God's character. The Scriptures emphasize no other qualities more than God's perfection and exaltation. We must appreciate this attribute to appreciate God.

Student Work

The Importance of God's Holiness

God's Holiness Is Honored Above Every Other Attribute

Holiness Alone Is Expressed Three-Fold

✎ Read Isaiah 6:3 and Revelation 4:8. Write the triple declaration presented in both of these verses. _____

Elsewhere in the Scriptures, we can find similar three-fold expressions— as when God foretold ruin and destruction for those who rejected Him (Ezek. 21:27).

No other attribute of God is honored in this way. We do not read that God is "eternal, eternal, eternal" or "almighty, almighty, almighty."

Holiness Alone Is the Attribute by Which God Swears

Read Psalm 89:35. God promises with His holiness as an assurance, because His holiness is the attribute that most clearly identifies Him.

In Hebrews we read that when God made a covenant with Abraham, He swore by Himself (Heb. 6:13–18), since there could be no greater authority or assurance. Therefore, when we read that God swears by His holiness, we can see that this attribute is tied closely with His core identity.

Holiness Is His Glory and Beauty

Read Psalm 29:1–2. God's holiness is wondrous. It shines with the beauty and glory that sets Him apart from everything and everyone else in the universe. He has attributes and power that no one else has. He reigns from the highest peak of perfection, and we stagger to crane our necks to catch a glimpse of that majesty.

God's Holiness Is the Glory of Every Other Attribute

Holiness is the splendor of every attribute in the Godhead. His justice is a *holy* justice; His omniscience is a *holy* omniscience; His power is a *holy* power (Ps. 98:1); and His promises are *holy* promises.

Imagine all these attributes if they were not holy. Without holiness, His patience would be an indulgence to sin. His mercy might seem like a fondness for sin. His wrath would be arbitrary madness. If God was not perfect and exalted, we might have reason to call His power tyranny, or His wisdom falsehood.

But God is the *best*—He meets and exceeds every good standard. He indeed *is* the standard for everyone else.

A Definition of Holiness

What is holiness? Our definition can benefit from a study of the root word from which we translate the English word *holy*.

The Derivative of the Word Holiness

The Old Testament word for *holy* comes from the Hebrew root word *qodhesh*, meaning "apartness, separateness." It derives from the root word *qod*, meaning "to cut."

The New Testament word for *holy* comes from the Greek word *hagios*, meaning "to set apart for a particular service."

Of course, languages grow and change, so scholars cannot always define the full meaning of a term by the meaning of its root. However, the frequent use of the word *holiness* in the Bible gives us enough context for a clear definition.

The Two-Fold Definition

As discussed in the first lesson, holiness includes two broad ideas:

- **Defined Negatively**—Holiness is perfection. It is a separation *from* sin.

- **Defined Positively**—Holiness is exaltation. It is a separation *to* some higher position, state, or purpose.

When discussing holiness, we must keep both ideas in mind. We cannot reflect holiness simply by cutting off contact with people and things that we think are bad. Likewise, we cannot pursue God's purpose unless we reject sin.

Understanding God's Holiness

As we apply these two ideas to the holiness of God, we see two main truths.

God Is Absolutely Pure

He is completely separate from sin, and it is impossible that He would commit sin. God *is* light, and in Him is no darkness at all (1 John 1:5). He stands removed from even the touch or sight of sin (Hab. 1:13).

God Is Exalted Above All Else

As we read in Isaiah 57:15, God's identity is holiness. He is high and exalted above all things. Of course, this is also true of both the Spirit and the Son.

Understanding Our Holiness

Likewise, God has sanctified believers *from* sin and *to* Himself.

God's Holiness Bars Our Sin from His Presence

✎ According to Revelation 21:27, what will not enter God's New Jerusalem in the world to come?

_____

_____

_____

_____

God will not allow sin or sinful people into the presence of His glory. Anyone in His new Creation must be purified by Christ.

God Gives Us Holiness Through His Son

✎ When Christ hung on the cross, what did He cry out to God (Mark 15:34)?

_____

_____

✎ In Psalm 22:1–3, what answer do we find to this question (v. 3)?

_____

God somehow tore Himself apart so that we could be one with Him. He became what was repugnant to Him so that we could become righteous.

✎ Write 2 Corinthians 5:21 below:

_____

_____

_____

_____

_____

Sin corrupted God's Creation, but in His holiness and love, He acted to redeem those who would trust in Him. He became our sin so that we could become His righteousness.

This motive of love helps us understand Isaiah 53:10–12. Read this passage, and answer the following questions:

✎ What was the pleasure, or will, of the Lord (v. 10)?

_____

✎ What satisfied the Lord (v. 11)?

_____

At first glance, this passage makes God seem cruel and heartless. But now we understand that the Son's death made many people righteous (v. 11), and through this sacrifice He became the mediator for sinners (v. 12). In Christ's death, we see the perfect, harmonious expression of God's love, power, and righteousness, whereby He suffered an act of cruelty against Himself and transformed it into an act of salvation for us.

✎ Read Hebrews 2:14–15.

- What did Christ destroy through His death?

  _____

- What fear did Christ therefore remove? What fear kept us in slavery?

  _____

If we trust in Christ, God removes us from the power of sin, setting us apart to His righteousness, His service, and His care.

God Continues to Make Us More Holy

God *sanctified* us—that is, set us apart—at the moment of our salvation, but He continues to sanctify us as we grow in love and knowledge.

✎ Again, what command do we find in 1 Peter 1:15–16?

_____

We mirror God's holiness by rejecting sin and clinging to Him.

Separation from Sin

Read Romans 13:12–14.

✎ What should we throw away (v. 12)?

_____

✎ What examples of this are listed in verse 13?

_____

_____

_____

✎ Explain in your own words the command given in verse 14.

_____

_____

_____

_____

_____

Ask God to put you far from anything that would betray His love. Mirror the thoughts and behavior of Christ, and you will reject opportunities to sin.

Separation to God

Read Romans 12:1–2.

✏ By what gift of God does Paul make this appeal?

_____

✏ How does Paul describe our "living sacrifice"?

_____

_____

We are now dead to sin, but alive to God (Rom. 6:11). We are still imperfect, but God continues to sanctify us for His good purpose. We have but to follow His leading.

Read 2 Timothy 2:20–26, where Paul compares believers to vessels—that is, containers or jars. God's grace flows into us, and as we abide in Him, that grace overflows into the lives of other people.

✏ How then can we be more useful vessels for God? In your own words, summarize the advice Paul gave to Timothy in each of the following verses:

- Verse 22—_____

_____

_____

_____

- Verse 23—_____

_____

_____

_____

- Verse 24—_____

_____

_____

_____

- Verses 25–26—_____

_____

_____

_____

Notes from the Teacher's Lesson

As you listen to the Teacher's Lesson, record your thoughts on the following passages.

- Psalm 111:9

  _____

  _____

- 1 John 1:5

  _____

  _____

- Isaiah 6:1

  _____

  _____

- Isaiah 6:2

  _____

  _____

- Isaiah 6:3

  _____

  _____

- Isaiah 6:4

  _____

  _____

Application Activities

1. Evaluate and explain the following statement in three paragraphs: "We cannot worship God without appreciating His holiness."

2. In what ways did Christ reveal His divine holiness, even though He was human? Cite at least three examples from His life and ministry.

3. Read each of the verses in the following table. Write in the right column what the passage says we *are* because of Christ. Then choose three of these examples, and explain how you believe we should express that identity. What does Scripture say that we should do to reflect God?

Passage	Because of Christ, I Am . . .
Matthew 5:13	
Matthew 5:14	
1 Corinthians 3:16	
1 Corinthians 12:27	
Ephesians 2:10	
Ephesians 2:19	
1 Peter 2:5	
1 Peter 2:9–10	
1 Peter 2:11	

4. The following passages teach us many things about God's holiness. Read each verse, and briefly note your thoughts on its lessons.

Exodus 3:5	Psalm 18:30	Isaiah 5:16	Habakkuk 1:12
Exodus 15:11	Psalm 22:3	Isaiah 6:3	Matthew 5:48
Leviticus 19:2	Psalm 30:4	Isaiah 12:6	Matthew 19:17
Deuteronomy 32:4	Isaiah 29:19	Luke 1:49	Joshua 24:19
Psalm 36:6	Isaiah 43:14	1 Samuel 2:2	Psalm 47:8
Isaiah 45:19	John 17:11	1 Samuel 6:20	Psalm 48:1
Isaiah 47:4	Romans 1:23	1 Chronicles 16:10	Psalm 60:6
Isaiah 49:7	Hebrews 1:8	Job 4:17	Psalm 89:35
Isaiah 52:10	James 1:13	Job 6:10	Psalm 92:15
Isaiah 57:15	1 Peter 1:15	Psalm 99:3	Jeremiah 2:5
1 John 1:5	Job 25:5	Psalm 111:9	Lamentations 3:38
1 John 2:20	Job 34:10	Psalm 119:142	Revelation 4:8
Job 36:23	Psalm 145:17	Revelation 6:10	Psalm 11:7
Proverbs 9:10	Hosea 11:9	Revelation 15:4	

CHAPTER 17

His Justice and Righteousness

"God cannot but be just. His holiness is the cause of His justice. Holiness will not suffer Him to do anything but what is righteous. He can no more be unjust than He can be unholy."

—Thomas Watson, *A Body of Divinity*

A college student, home for Christmas vacation, was driving her parents to church on a dark Sunday night. Just as they rounded the curve at the top of a hill, another car flew sideways over the hill from the other direction. The student had no time to react—the cars smashed together with a crunch of twisting metal.

The man driving the other car received only minor injuries. A woman who lived in a nearby house heard the collision and ran out in time to see the man move from the driver's seat to the passenger side of the car. He later told police officers that a friend had been driving—one who supposedly ran away after the accident. The witness, however, testified that no one else had been in the car. Officers found several recently emptied beer cans and liquor bottles on the floor of the car, but they didn't need these to prove that the man was drunk. They confiscated his driver's license and sent him to the hospital, where he was treated and released.

The student's mother, however, suffered serious injuries. The father was also in critical condition, and the student was little better. Her two brothers rushed to the hospital, and while their parents received emergency operations, they saw the police allow the drunk driver to leave the hospital, with hardly a scratch from the wreck.

Two days later, their mother died, never having regained consciousness. Her husband, injured so badly that he couldn't attend her funeral, remained in the hospital for several more weeks. The student, after enduring months of physical therapy, reluctantly left her father in the care of her relatives to resume her studies.

The chief investigating officer dragged his feet on the case, and the sheriff refused to push for a speedy prosecution. A judge refused to issue an arrest warrant for the drunk driver, in spite of testimony by multiple witnesses that he had bragged in a local bar about killing a woman and getting away without charges.

Where was God in all of this? How could He allow such flagrant injustice to go unchecked and unpunished? How could a God who allowed such a travesty be called loving?

God *is* just. He does punish evil and wickedness. But as temporal creatures, we are impatient. We want our eternal, transcendent God to exact justice *now*. But His justice is complete and perfect—not always fast.

Months passed following the family's tragedy. The daughter still hobbled painfully around the campus, attending her classes and focusing on her studies as best as she could. Her father, a self-employed contractor, was out of work for nearly a year, with little income to pay his expenses. The other driver had no active insurance, and since no charges had been filed, the family's own insurance company refused to pay their claims. The father had to meet them in court to force payment.

Worst of all, he missed his wife dearly. He tried to escape the hurt by immersing himself in the children's class that he and his wife had taught for many years. And he channeled his pain by writing letters and articles about his experience, encouraging politicians and community leaders to raise awareness about driving under the influence. Seeing his daughter happily married a few years later helped him appreciate the joys still remaining in his life.

It wasn't long before the city held local elections, and the sheriff sought re-election. His opponent ran a tough campaign, focusing on the need for tougher enforcement of drunk-driving laws. The challenger won by a landslide.

In one of his first acts of office, the new sheriff conducted a routine investigation of all department personnel. His search revealed that the officer who refused to investigate the family's accident had lied on his employment application. He was immediately fired.

A few months after the former sheriff left office, he was arrested, tried, convicted of masterminding a drug ring and a chop-shop operation. He had used his access to evidence lockers to sell drugs and car parts. A judge sentenced him to twenty years in prison.

The drunk driver, who never sought help for his addiction, committed suicide several years later. The guilt of his actions never left him.

There is no sin on Earth that will not be corrected in heaven. Even if we do not see all the consequences for sin in this life, we will in the life to come. We are all corrupt, sin-drunk killers, guilty of the death of Christ, and we all deserve an eternity without Him. And without the grace of God, we all face a day of judgment from which we have no escape.

But God executed His justice on Himself, so that we could receive pardon and freedom from our sin. And as we look out on a world of chaos and injustice today, we can pursue justice in His name, trusting Him to work for our good and for His glory.

Student Work

✎ Summarize what the following verses teach about God's justice.

- Psalm 19:9

_____

_____

_____

- Psalm 145:17

_____

_____

_____

The immediate implication of God's justice is His judgment of humanity. All of us are sinners, and God will execute complete and perfect justice. Without Christ, this knowledge could terrify us. With Him, it humbles and inspires us.

Our Guilt Under God's Justice

Read Acts 17:30–31, and answer the following questions.

- When will God judge the world?
  _____
  _____

- When therefore should people repent? _____

- By whom will He judge the world?
  _____
  _____
  _____

Christ is the standard by which God will judge all the people of the world. Everyone who cannot match His righteousness will perish.

- Write Romans 3:23 below:
  _____
  _____
  _____

In what ways do we fall short?

We Fall Short of His Holiness

- Read Mark 1:23–25. What did the demon acknowledge Jesus to be?
  _____

- How does Hebrews 7:26 describe the holiness of Christ?
  _____
  _____
  _____
  _____

  Can we match that standard? _____

We Fall Short of His Judgment

✎ In John 8:16, how did Jesus describe His judgment?

_____

_____

_____

Can we judge with the same perspective, clarity, and wisdom as this?
_____

We do not always see things exactly as they are. Our perspective and judgment is clouded by sin and weakness. We therefore depend on Christ for righteousness and strength. He is always true and never false.

We Fall Short of His Speech

✎ According to 1 Peter 2:22, what was true of Christ's speech?

_____

_____

Can the same be said of any of us? _____

We Fall Short of His Mercy

✎ According to 1 Peter 2:23, how did Christ react to mistreatment?

_____

_____

_____

Have we always responded perfectly to mistreatment? _____

We Fall Short of His Unity with the Father

✎ According to Christ's statement in John 8:29, how often did His actions please God the Father? _____

✎ How did He reveal His submission in Luke 22:42?

_____

_____

_____

✎ Read Philippians 2:5–8. To what point was Christ obedient?

_____

Though Christ knew exactly the suffering that He'd face on the cross, He chose to put away any fear or instinct to run. Instead, He kept His will in perfect alignment with the Father's—and in so doing, He became the perfect example of submission. None of us can yet claim this same unity with the Father.

Remember: God will judge every person by this perfect standard.

Christ's Righteousness Is Now Ours

Thankfully, Christ offers His righteousness to all who trust Him. It is just and right for God to allow those people into heaven.

✎ By nature, we all fall short of God's righteous requirements (Rom. 3:23), and we can do nothing to change this. Write Romans 8:8 below:

_____

_____

_____

_____

Christ therefore took our place, thereby . . .

- Paying the penalty for our sin with His death
- Fulfilling God's standard of a perfect, holy sacrifice

Now that we have accepted Christ, He has _become_ our righteousness (1 Cor. 1:30), and His righteousness is credited in full to our account (Rom. 4:6, 11, 23–24). When God looks at us now, He chooses not to see our sin, but rather Christ's perfection. We can now be that holy, acceptable, and _living_ sacrifice (Rom. 12:1).

✎ Read Romans 3:26. What two things has God shown Himself to be?

- He is _____.

- He is the _____ of those who have faith in Christ.

Through Christ's sacrifice, God saves us while still expressing perfect justice. There is no contradiction between His justice and His mercy.

Notes from the Teacher's Lesson

The Definition of Justice and Righteousness

_____

_____

_____

_____

The Statement of Justice and Righteousness

_____

Questioning God's Justice

Examples of God's justice:

- _____ (Lev. 10:1–2)

- _____ (2 Sam. 6:5–11; Num. 4:15, 19–20)

The Conquest of Canaan

- The Justification (Gen. 18:25; Ps. 9:8; James 4:12):

  _____

  _____

  _____

  _____

- The Context – Summarize the points brought up by your teacher in your class discussion:

  ○ _____

  _____

  _____

  _____

  ○ _____

  _____

  _____

  _____

Application Activities

1. Read and meditate on Romans 2:1–16. List everything you see about the justice of God, especially in contrast to humanity.

2. Meditate on the justice of God in His providence. Record a providence that displays the justice of God in His dealings with people. You can draw an example from any category, whether biblical, personal, or otherwise.

3. Memorize and meditate on Jeremiah 9:24.

4. List any personal problems or injustices that you are praying for God to resolve. Pray that you would see God's justice, but pray also that God would give you patience in the meantime. Ask Him also for the strength to show mercy and love, as appropriate.

5. Describe two examples of injustice, one for each category below. Explain why you believe that each example belongs in the given category.

   A. Injustices that Christians should wait for God to resolve.

   B. Injustices that Christians should seek to resolve themselves while reflecting God's love and truth.

6. In a page or less, briefly summarize one argument made by a theologian or philosopher to answer the *problem of evil*. In what ways is this answer—called a *theodicy*—helpful? Likewise, how is it insufficient? Cite any sources that you use.

CHAPTER 18

His Mercy and Grace

"Of all God's attributes, mercy is the crown."

—Andrew Murray, *God's Best Secrets*

The poet Frederick William Faber penned the following in 1854:

> There's a wideness in God's mercy,
> Like a wideness of the sea;
> There's a kindness in His justice,
> Which is more than liberty.

God's mercy had touched the life of Faber, and he wanted to share its truth with others—so much, actually, that he wrote twelve verses.

A high school senior named Lizzie S. Tourjée wrote a musical score for the poem in 1878, to be performed at her graduation. As the daughter of Eben Tourjée, she had developed her talent over many years, and her delicate melody turned Faber's poem into a much-loved hymn.

The text celebrates the mercy of God given to us, sinners, who deserve only His wrath. And much more than that, we find the grace to sustain us in this life—and the hope of immeasurable goodness in the eternity beyond.

> There is welcome for the sinner,
> And more graces for the good;
> There is mercy with the Savior;
> There is healing in His blood.
>
> There is grace enough for thousands
> Of new worlds as great as this;

There is room for fresh creations
In that upper home of bliss.

For the love of God is broader
Than the measure of our mind;
And the heart of the Eternal
Is most wonderfully kind.

These gifts encourage us to cling to God, and they inspire us to share His love with others.

Souls of men! why will ye scatter
Like a crowd of frightened sheep?
Foolish hearts! why will ye wander
From a love so true and deep?

It is God: His love looks mighty,
But is mightier than it seems;
'Tis our Father: and His fondness
Goes far out beyond our dreams.

But we make His love too narrow
By false limits of our own;
And we magnify His strictness
With a zeal He will not own.

Was there ever kinder shepherd
Half so gentle, half so sweet,
As the Savior who would have us
Come and gather at His feet?

Student Work

God's Goodness

Mercy and Grace

Mercy is not receiving the bad we deserve. Grace is receiving the good we don't deserve. By God's mercy, He saves us from hell, and by His grace, He redeems us to heaven.

Mercy is one form of God's goodness (Ps. 23:6)—specifically, the goodness of salvation, which we do not and could not deserve. Likewise, grace is His goodness shown in the life of a believer. God is merciful and gracious because He is good.

Goodness Is Part of God's Glory

✎ Read Exodus 33:18–19. What did Moses ask to see?

_____

✎ What three things did God tell Moses He would show him?

- God would make His _____ pass in front of Moses.

- God would proclaim His _____.

- God would be gracious and show _____ to those He chose.

This is God's glory—this is His love and truth. He glorifies Himself by making Himself known and by saving His people.

God's Goodness Is Free

Mercy is, by definition, given to those who do not deserve it. Goodness offered to people who *do* deserve it—like payment or gifts of thanks—is not what we find in salvation. God owes us nothing, nor does He need anything from us.

Mercy is therefore free, as is all the grace of God. To accept His gifts, we need only draw close to Him—again, not because He needs something from us, but because He chooses to shine His light through a relationship with Him.

✎ Read the passages below, and fill in the blanks.

- We are _____ freely by His grace (Rom. 3:24).

- With Christ, God will give us _____ (Rom. 8:32).

- He _____ us, not because of anything good we did, but because of His mercy (Titus 3:5).

- From God we can freely take the water of _____ (Rev. 22:17).

God's Goodness Is Infinite

There are no bounds or limits to God's mercy to His children. His mercy is . . .

- Plentiful, abundant (Ps. 86:5)
- Great—God is "rich in mercy" (Eph. 2:4)
- New every morning (Lam. 3:22–23)

✎ Write Lamentations 3:22–23 below:

_____

_____

_____

_____

_____

_____

God's Goodness Is Eternal

✎ How does Psalm 103:17 describe God's mercy, or steadfast love? From _____ to _____.

✎ How many times does Psalm 136 speak of His mercy, or steadfast love? _____

God's mercy does not arise from a temporary mood. It is a permanent expression of His being—like His love and holiness. As long as He is God, He will be merciful.

All Goodness Is Derived from God

✍ What title does Paul ascribe to God the Father in 2 Corinthians 1:3?

_____

From God comes all good things (James 1:17), including the very idea of mercy. The only reason we can offer up goodness to others is because God first showed His goodness to us. As Christ commanded in Luke 6:36, we should be merciful, just as our Father is merciful.

God's Mercy Is Personified in Christ

In His earthly ministry, Christ stopped to respond to people who pleaded for His mercy. He healed two blind men who cried after Him (Matt. 9:27–30). He healed the daughter of a Canaanite woman who persisted in seeking mercy (Matt. 15:22–28). And in the ultimate act of mercy, He died for all of us.

✍ Write Romans 5:6 below:

_____

_____

_____

And through the resurrection of Christ, we have a new life and a new hope of a future with God. This too is an act of mercy (1 Pet. 1:3).

We Now Live in Grace

God's mercy unlocked His grace to us. As believers, we are now dead to sin, but alive in Christ (Gal. 2:20). We are free from the bondage of sin and the Law, and we now have the liberty to reflect God's love and truth. We have direct access to His wisdom, His strength, His truth, His Spirit, and His hope.

Even though we can still fail and sin, we need not worry about provoking God's wrath. God loves us, and as discussed in previous lessons, He will keep us secure until the day we see Him face-to-face. This is not a license to sin—but rather a challenge to live in gratitude for His goodness.

Notes from the Teacher's Lesson

The Definitions of Mercy and Grace

- God in His mercy . . .

  _____

  _____

- God in His grace . . .

  _____

  _____

The Statements of Mercy and Grace

_____

The Significance of Mercy and Grace *(Matt. 18:21–35)*

- God's mercy and grace to _____ (vv. 21–27)
- Our mercy and grace to _____ (vv. 28–35)

What Is Forgiveness?

- *Forgiveness* is . . .

  _____

  _____

  _____

- *Reconciliation* is . . .

  _____

  _____

  _____

How to Forgive *(Matt. 18:15–20)*

- _____ what made the relationship break down.
- _____ any of your sin to God.
- _____ to forgive the other person.

- _____ from the other person, if applicable.

- _____ the person to fellowship, if possible.

  - **Attempt 1:** Try to resolve the issue with the offender privately (v. 15).

  - **Attempt 2:** Try to resolve the issue again, but with one or two witnesses present (v. 16).

  - **Attempt 3:** Tell the church about the offense, and let the assembly address the offender (v. 17).

  - **Attempt 4:** Treat the offender as if he or she were an unbeliever—that is, someone who needs the grace of the gospel (v. 17).

Additional Notes on Forgiveness

- Be humble (Gal. 6:1–2).

- Don't take offense too easily (1 Pet. 4:8).

- Externalize the problem and treasure the person (Gal. 3:13).

- Prevent further harm and alert appropriate authorities (Prov. 24:11; Rom. 13:1–5).

Application Activities

1. Read and meditate on God's mercies in Psalm 136. In your own words, record how God's mercy manifests in each verse, as grouped under the following categories.

   A. His person (vv. 1–3)

   B. His power (vv. 4–9)

   C. His past history (vv. 10–24)

   D. His providences (v. 25)

2. Read and meditate on God's providences in Psalm 103. From the psalm, answer the following questions.

   A. What should we not forget?

   B. What is our crown?

   C. How does verse 10 describe God's mercy?

   D. What would God do if He gave us what we deserve?

   E. How great is God's mercy?

   F. To whom is God's mercy offered?

   G. How does verse 12 describe God's mercy?

   H. How long will His mercy last?

3. Cite a providence—either in your life or in a contemporary's—in which God gave mercy when wrath was deserved.

4. Describe a past wrong—big or small—committed against you or someone you know. Change the names in your description as appropriate. Using the principles offered in this lesson, describe how the offended person might reach out in forgiveness or reconciliation to the offender.

   A. What role does God's grace play in this process?

   B. Is personal safety an issue?

   C. What about legal consequences?

   D. Is full reconciliation possible in this case?

5. Read Charles Haddon Spurgeon's book *All of Grace*.

   - In two pages or less, summarize the lessons you learn from your reading. Include brief quotations as necessary.

   - List any examples of God's grace that you find helpful.

6. Reflect on some of God's grace in your life.

   - Make a list of people who have been gracious to you. Beside each name, write a brief description of their grace.

   - Next, make a list of people to whom you can reflect the same kind of grace, especially those that others seem to ignore. Beside each name, write down practical ways in which you can be gracious to them.

   - Then *reach out*!

CHAPTER 19

His Love

"The Christian . . . does not think God will love us because we are good, but that God will make us good because He loves us . . ."

—C.S. Lewis, *Mere Christianity*

In 1919, Frederick Martin Lehman wrote a hymn that summarizes the central message discussed in this lesson—the love of God. Lehman adapted the words to his hymn from a Jewish poem, "Hadamut," which was written in Aramaic in 1050 by Meir Ben Isaac Nehorai of Worms, Germany. Lehman's daughter, Claudia Mays, arranged the music.

The history and themes behind this hymn reflect a broad array of cultures—which is appropriate, since God's love reaches beyond human-made boundaries to people of all nations, backgrounds, and languages. We humans may seem very different, but we share the same image of God and the same need for His redemptive grace.

The love of God is greater far
Than tongue or pen can ever tell;
It goes beyond the highest star,
And reaches to the lowest hell.

The guilty pair, bowed down with care,
God gave His Son to win;
His erring child He reconciled,
And pardoned from his sin.

When years of time shall pass away,
And earthly thrones and kingdoms fall,

When men, who here refuse to pray,
On rocks and hills and mountains call,

God's love so sure, shall still endure,
All measureless and strong;
Redeeming grace to Adam's race—
The saints' and angels' song.

Could we with ink the ocean fill,
And were the skies of parchment made,
Were every stalk on earth a quill,
And every man a scribe by trade,

To write the love of God above,
Would drain the ocean dry.
Nor could the scroll contain the whole,
Though stretched from sky to sky.

In our attempts to describe the love of God, we are like ants holding up grains of sand, trying to picture in our tiny minds the scope of the Himalayas. His love stretches so much higher and deeper and beyond our understanding. We cannot yet glimpse its full grandeur, because we do not yet have the perspective that eternity will give us.

O love of God, how rich and pure!
How measureless and strong!
It shall for evermore endure
The saints' and angels' song.

As Tozer wrote about God's love, "I can no more do justice to that awesome and wonder-filled theme than a child can grasp a star. Still, by reaching toward the star, the child may call attention to it."

Therefore, with a sense of awe and inadequacy, we focus our attention on this vast, incomprehensible attribute of God.

Student Work

Our Love for God

We cannot study God's love for us without soon realizing that our own love for Him, in comparison, is pitiful and weak. We strain even to say that it is the same type of love. After all, what good can we offer God that He did not first give to us? God did not benefit from loving us, yet He chose to do so anyway. He chose to offer us mercy, to establish a relationship with us, and to shower us with His grace.

The Basis of Our Love

As 1 John 4:19 teaches us, we love because He first loved us. Even if we defined love merely as an *attraction* to good, who but God deserves our love most? When we behold the beauty, glory, and grace of God, how can we do anything but love Him?

We must know God to love Him. We must understand and appreciate His innate goodness, and we must meditate on all the gifts He's given us. As Thomas Watson wrote:

> The antecedent of love is knowledge. The Spirit shines upon the understanding, and [reveals] the beauties of wisdom, holiness, and mercy in God; and these are the loadstone to entice and draw out love to God. [People who] know not God cannot love Him; if the sun be set in the understanding, there must needs be night in the affections.

✐ Read Psalm 37:1–4. Instead of worrying about the wrongs committed by others, what should we do (vv. 3–4)?

_____

_____

_____

As we take time to appreciate all the good things God has given us, we will learn to delight in Him. We will put aside fear and worry, instead trusting God's faithfulness to us.

The Nature of Our Love

Note the following qualities that the Spirit develops within a sincere love for God.

We Love God First with All of Our Self

✎ Read Matthew 22:35–37. With what are we to love God?

_____

_____

God asks for all of us. We cannot divide our service between Him and any other master (Matt. 6:24). God is the only One we should worship (Exo. 20:1–4), and He is the One we should love above all else.

And we should love Him intensely. Our entire being should radiate with love for Him. This love should infuse all of our thoughts, words, and actions.

When we love God, we learn to love what He loves—and hate what He hates (Rom. 12:9). We despise sin, but seek good for sinners. We love God first, but we also love others as much as we love ourselves (Matt. 22:39). We learn to appreciate God's image in *all* people. This perspective changes who we are and how we treat others.

We Love God Himself

We do not love God just because He gives good things to us. We love Him for who He *is*. All His gifts simply reveal facets of His character.

This kind of focused love allows us to trust Him even when life seems to fall apart—even when we don't seem to have many good things around us. And as we love God for His power, holiness, and grace, He will give us the faith and hope we need.

✎ Read Psalm 18:1–3, and list what God is to us:

_____

_____

_____

_____

✎ Read Psalm 42:1–3. Describe in your own words the love the psalmist expresses for God.

_____

_____

_____

_____

The psalmist cannot bear the thought of living without God. If this were a relationship between two humans, we might call it unhealthy or co-dependent. But remember that from God comes *all goodness*. There is no light or truth or goodness apart from Him. If we could somehow completely shut Him out from our lives, we would find ourselves, quite literally, in hell.

We can therefore understand the pain that Christ experienced when God turned away from Him at the cross (Matt. 27:46), and the sorrow felt by Mary Magdalene when she could not even find Jesus' body at the tomb (John 20:13).

We cannot separate any of God's gifts from His Person. If we desire any good at all, we desire *Him*.

We Love God Actively

As discussed in the teacher's lesson for this chapter, love is not merely passive attraction—it is a decision to act. Feelings may or may not follow.

✎ Read John 14:15. What does Christ expect of those who say they love Him?

_____

_____

Why? Because those who delight in His character should seek to reflect it. If we appreciate His holiness, mercy, and love, we should—by His grace—be holy, merciful, and loving.

This does not mean that work itself *is* love. As we learn from 1 Corinthians 13, we can make acts of service and sacrifice without love. Likewise, love isn't *all* work. Christ taught that hardship awaited those who followed Him, but He will also give us rest. The burden of learning from Him is light (Matt. 11:25–30).

Labor does, however, result from true love. It can take work to serve another person. But as a loving parent or spouse might tell you, service does not always feel like hard work when done for someone you love.

✎ Read John 12:1–8, and answer the following questions:

- What good had Jesus done for these three siblings (v. 1)?
  _____
  _____

- How did Mary express her love for Jesus (v. 3)?
  _____
  _____
  _____

- Why did Judas say he was upset (v. 5)?
  _____
  _____
  _____

- Why was he *actually* upset (v. 6)?
  _____
  _____

- What do you think Christ meant by what He said in verses 7–8?
  _____
  _____
  _____
  _____
  _____

What distinguished Mary from Judas? What made Mary disregard the value of the perfume Judas thought so precious? Her love for Jesus.

We Love God Steadfastly

Trials and hardships will test our love. This is why Paul prayed that the Spirit would give the Ephesian believers strength (Eph. 3:14–19).

✎ In what should we be rooted and grounded (v. 17)? _____

✏ What will that in turn help us know (v. 19)?

_____

God's love for us does not weaken. And as long as our love is built upon His love, we will not stop loving, either.

✏ Write 1 Corinthians 13:7 below:

_____

_____

_____

_____

Every person's greatest need is to know God. And His love compels this relationship more than anything else. Therefore, if we truly love God, we should strive to connect others to His love.

- When we tell unbelievers how Christ helped the hurt and the rejected, they should find a ready example of such service in us (James 1:27).
- When we describe Christ's anger at religious leaders and hypocrites, unbelievers should not have reason to believe that we're hypocritical (Matt. 7:5).
- When we tell unbelievers of Christ's sacrifice, they should see us living out a sacrifice for Him (Rom. 12:1).

Unbelievers should not struggle to imagine what Christ's love might be like. They should see Him shining clearly, consistently, and steadfastly through us.

Notes from the Teacher's Lesson

The Definition of Love

- What love is:

  _____

  _____

  - Love recognizes the good that God placed *in* others.

  - Love seeks God's good *for* others.

- What love is not:

  - Love is not _____

  - Love is not _____

  - Love is not _____

  - Love is not _____

The Statement of God's Love

_____

- God the _____ of love (v. 7)

- God the _____ of love (v. 8)

God's Attribute	The Attribute's Expression with Love
	God loved us before the foundation of the world— and not for anything we did (Eph. 1:4).
	God will love us forever (Ps. 100:5).
	God's love is true, equitable, and offered to all (Ps. 116:5; John 3:16).
	God's love is great and boundless (Eph. 2:4–7).
	God's love is spotlessly pure (John 14:15; 1 John 4:18).

God's Attribute	The Attribute's Expression with Love
	God loves us despite His perfect knowledge of our sin (Rom. 7:24–25).
	God's love can reach us anywhere we go (Ps. 139).
	Nothing can separate us from God's love (Rom. 8:31–39).
	He loves us not because of anything we have done (Titus 3:5).
	God's love never changes (Ps. 136; Jer. 31:3).

- The manifestation of God's love (vv. 9–10):

  - God's love manifested through _____

  - His love manifested to _____

  - His love manifested to _____

The Significance of God's Love

- To _____ (1 John 4:10)

- To _____ (1 John 4:11)

  - The Path of Duty—resistance, resentment, relenting

  - The Path of Love—rejoicing, reflecting, rest

- To _____ (1 John 4:17–18)

Application Activities

1. Read and study 1 Corinthians 13, Paul's passage on godly love. Make a list of all of the characteristics of love found in that chapter. Beside each characteristic, write one practical application of that characteristic that a teenager can make at home.

2. Using the example of Christ and the characteristics listed in 1 Corinthians 13, write a two-page paper describing how a husband or wife can reflect godly love to his or her spouse. Cite at least three ways derived from Scripture.

3. Choose a song or poem, and write a three-paragraph paper summarizing its view on love. For a challenge, consider the poem "Love's Deity" by John Donne.

4. Read carefully the following two poems, "A Modest Love" and Sonnet 116.

   - For each poem, write a paragraph briefly summarizing its view or definition of love. Write your own analysis before consulting other works, but if you do rely on other sources, be sure to cite them. What good message could you find in each poem?

   - Then write a third paragraph explaining which poem you found more compelling, and why.

   - Finally, write a brief, concluding paragraph that states which of these poems you believe best reflects the kind of love of God has toward us. Or do you think both poems reflect different parts of the same love?

A Modest Love

By Sir Edward Dyer

The lowest trees have tops, the ant her gall,
   The fly her spleen, the little sparks their heat;
The slender hairs cast shadows, though but small,
   And bees have stings, although they be not great;
Seas have their source, and so have shallow springs;
And love is love, in beggars as in kings.

Where rivers smoothest run, deep are the fords;
   The dial stirs, yet none perceives it move;
The firmest faith is in the fewest words;
   The turtles cannot sing, and yet they love:
True hearts have eyes and ears, no tongues to speak;
They hear and see, and sigh, and then they break.

Sonnet 116

By William Shakespeare

Let me not to the marriage of true minds
Admit impediments. Love is not love
Which alters when it alteration finds,
Or bends with the remover to remove:
O no; it is an ever-fixed mark,
That looks on tempests, and is never shaken;
It is the star to every wandering bark,
Whose worth's unknown, although his height be taken.
Love's not Time's fool, though rosy lips and cheeks
Within his bending sickle's compass come;
Love alters not with his brief hours and weeks,
But bears it out even to the edge of doom.
If this be error and upon me proved,
I never writ, nor no man ever loved.

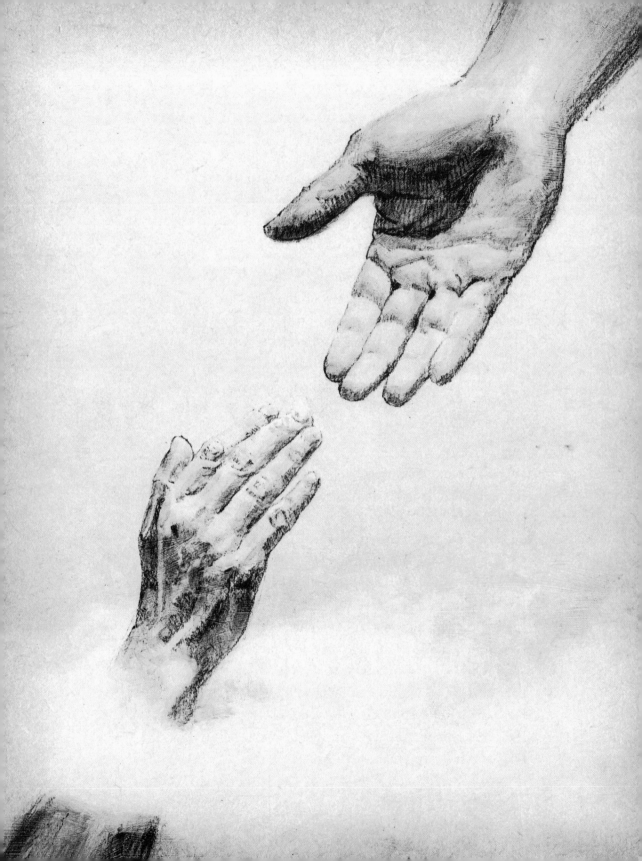

CHAPTER 20

Knowing God: A Review

"It is little comfort to know there is a God, unless He be ours. God offers Himself to be our God. And faith catches hold of the offer, it appropriates God, and makes all that is in Him over to us to be ours: His wisdom to be ours, to teach us; His holiness ours, to sanctify us; His Spirit ours, to comfort us; His mercy ours, to save us."

—Thomas Watson, *A Body of Divinity*

The following review questions can help you prepare for your third unit test. Given the length and complexity of Unit 3, you will likely benefit from extra study.

In addition to any extra material that your teacher provides, you should consult the notes from each teacher's lesson, as well as the major points from each chapter's student exercises.

. . . .

Review Questions

While the following questions may help you prepare, please note that the final test questions will differ. The test may cover the same material in different ways, or include topics not mentioned here. Your teacher may provide you with additional information.

✎ Name three things that, according to this study, "knowing God" is *not*.

- _____
- _____
- _____

✎ What do we mean by God's *essence*?

_____

_____

_____

✎ How is the meaning of *attribute* different from the meaning of *essence*?

_____

_____

_____

✎ Which attribute of God . . .

• Is seen in the name *El Shaddai*? _____

• Is seen in the phrase *La Hai Roi*? _____

• Is stated in 1 John 4:7–10? _____

• Is honored above all other attributes? _____

• Is stated in Exodus 34:6? _____

• Makes God in some way knowable and predictable? _____

✎ Describe the two-fold meaning of God's holiness.

_____

_____

✎ What is the difference between mercy and grace?

_____

_____

_____

_____

_____

✎ In Matthew 18, what four steps did Christ offer to restore a fellow believer to the assembly?

1. _____

_____

2. _____

_____

3. _____

_____

4. _____

_____

✎ Distinguish between forgiveness and reconciliation, as defined by this study.

_____

_____

_____

_____

_____

_____

✎ Define what love is. List also examples of what love is *not*.

_____

_____

_____

_____

✎ Over what powers or beings does God have absolute sovereignty? Give three examples from Scripture.

_____

_____

_____

_____

✎ List at least three names of God, along with their meanings.

_____

_____

_____

_____

✎ Which lesson in this unit meant the most to you? Why?

_____

_____

_____

_____

_____

_____

_____

_____

_____

_____

· ·

Notes from the Teacher's Lesson

God's Greatness *(Exo. 20:1–3)*

God's Goodness

- All people are _____ against a holy God (Rom. 3:23).

- All people deserve eternal _____ for their sin (Rom. 6:23).

- God loved us enough to take our punishment on Himself (John 3:16).

- Anyone who believes in Christ is _____ to God (Acts 16:30–31).

The Blessings of Our God

- Escape from the sting of _____ (1 Cor. 15:50–58)

- An eternal _____ (Ps. 119:57)

UNIT 4
The History of Christ

"If Jesus Christ was so abased for us, took our flesh, which was a disparagement to Him, mingling dust with gold, if He abased Himself so for us, let us be willing to be abased for Him."

—Thomas Watson, *A Body of Divinity*

CHAPTER 21

The Preciousness of Christ

"Jesus Christ, our Mediator, has perfection in every grace. . . . This no saint on Earth has; he may excel in one grace, but not in all; as Abraham was eminent for faith, Moses for meekness; but Christ excels in every grace."

—Thomas Watson, *A Body of Divinity*

Perhaps the greatest symbol of the British monarchy is the Crown Jewels. Representing both the wealth and the heritage of the royal family, this unrivaled collection has—in one form or another—accompanied kings and queens since at least the reign of King John (d. 1216).

The jewels do not appear at public ceremonies often. As perhaps the rarest and most expensive collection of precious gems in the world, they stay under extremely tight security. They feature some of the largest diamonds in the world, including the polished 530-carat Cullinan I and the cut 105-carat Koh-i-Noor. The entire collection is considered priceless, but it's likely insured for several billion British pounds.

The jewels were not always held so tightly as they are today. Some chronicles say that King John lost many of them in quicksand in 1216, the same year the Magna Carta was signed. In the 1300s, the jewels remained hidden in secret chambers under the Tower of London. Edward III, however, pawned them to pay troop salaries—a practice forbidden after the jewels' recovery. But the wife of Charles I, Queen Henrietta Maria, pawned them again to finance her armies during the English Civil War (1642–1651).

When the Parliamentarians won the war against the Royalists, the victors did not consider the gems so priceless. After abolishing the monarchy and executing Charles I, Oliver Cromwell (d. 1658) destroyed or sold what remained of the collection. A controversial leader, Cromwell despised the throne and felt that the jewels represented the worst excesses of the monarchy.

But with the restoration of the monarchy under Charles II, the crown reassembled and remade its regalia. Later kings and queens would buy or otherwise acquire precious stones from around the world, leaving the royals with the collection they have now.

Today, visitors can see some of the collection on display in a highly secure museum in the Tower of London. Significant physical security and unspecified technology keep the gems and regalia visible, yet very far from the hands of would-be thieves. The royal family and the British people spare little expense to preserve and protect these symbols.

Believers, too, have a Crown Jewel—our Savior and Lord, Jesus Christ. His worth far outweighs any sparkling pile of cut rocks. But how much are we willing to sacrifice for Him? Do we keep Him secreted away as some hidden part of our identity, or do we display His truth and love proudly? He represents the uncorrupted love of our God—and the hope of His kingdom to come.

We begin our study of Christ by considering His value. From 1 Peter 2:4–7, we learn that He is precious and valuable—indeed, the very cornerstone of our faith.

Student Work

Read 2 Corinthians 5:11–6:13, and answer the following questions.

In 5:11–13, Paul explains that he and his fellow laborers share the gospel to honor God and serve His people—even if they might be called insane for doing so.

✎ According to verse 14, what therefore drives our ministry? _____

✎ How can believers then respond to the death of Christ (v. 15)?

_____

_____

_____

_____

✎ And what should we no longer do (v. 16)?

_____

_____

As children of God, we are new (v. 17). We're no longer bound to serve sin and death. We are spiritual beings, and we should reach out to others in love, recognizing that they, too, are image-bearers of God, people who will spend eternity somewhere.

✎ This new perspective comes from God, who reconciled us to Himself, thereby giving us the ministry of _____ (v. 18).

This is our work in the world. Because Christ showed us God's love and truth, we can help lead others back to God, as well.

✎ What job or role does Paul use in verse 20 to picture this ministry?

_____

Christ represents us before God, so we represent Him to the world. Therefore, we should not receive God's grace in vain—we must accept it, live in it, and share it with others (6:1). Why? Because *now* is the time of our salvation (v. 2). We live in the age of grace, where anyone can instantly receive salvation from God by simply trusting Christ.

✎ To pursue this work, therefore, what should we *not* do (v. 3)?

_____

_____

Using verses 4–7, list every item you can find under the appropriate header in the following table.

What Opposes Our Ministry	What Aids Our Ministry

But God uses all of this to spread His gospel. When people honor or dishonor us, when they slander or praise us, when they treat us like imposters, strangers, or people who deserve death, sorrow, and poverty—we know that we have a Savior who knows us, redeems us, and gives His own life and wealth (vv. 8–10).

Paul and his fellow laborers reflected the love of Christ by opening their hearts wide to the believers at Corinth (v. 11). In the same way, we can show our love for Christ by cherishing His people. This kind of ministry will often be difficult, but through this work, we walk in step with the love of God.

Notes from the Teacher's Lesson

The Need for Love *(1 Cor. 13)*

- What is useless without love?

  _____

  _____

  _____

  _____

  _____

  _____

  _____

  _____

God's Grace to Us

- _____ blessings

- _____ blessings

- _____ blessings

Our Response *(1 Pet. 2:6–10)*

- Christ is not precious to . . .

  o _____ (1 Pet. 2:8)

  o _____

- Christ is precious to . . .

  ° Believers who _____
    —Note Mary (Luke 1:46–55) and Peter (Matt. 14:29).

  ° Believers who _____

God's Truth in Christ

Doctrines	References
	1 Corinthians 6:11
	2 Corinthians 5:19
	Ephesians 1:7
	Romans 8:38–39
	1 Corinthians 15:12–22
	Hebrews 10:19–20

God's Person in Christ (John 14:9–11)

. . . .

Application Activities

1. Meditate on Christ. In preparation, read John 1 slowly and carefully. Then think about Christ for thirty minutes, thanking Him for what you learn about His character and work in John 1. Write a short summary of your thoughts and reflections.

2. Record a providence—from any category—in which you find the presence or power of Christ important.

3. Research the script for the coronation of Queen Elizabeth in 1953. List at least five examples of religious references in the script, writing a brief summary of each.

4. Read Chapter 1 ("Seeing Christ's Glory") of *The Glory of Christ* by John Owen. Briefly summarize each of the four rewards Owen lists for those willing to study the glory of Christ.

CHAPTER 22

The Pre-Existence of Christ

"Christ is the everlasting Father . . . Does divine worship belong to the first Person in the Trinity? So it does to Christ."

—Thomas Watson, *A Body of Divinity*

Imagine talking with someone whom you assume—based on his appearance—is about your own age. During the course of the conversation, however, you begin to suspect that the person is much older than you. He talks about his father's childhood as if they had both grown up together. And even stranger, he talks about his grandfather and great-grandfather in the same way. You'd soon begin to think, *How can this be? This person must be insane!*

This might help you appreciate the confusion of the scribes and Pharisees in John 8. In this chapter, Christ taught the people about Himself, yet the religious leaders repeatedly tried to trip Him up with questions and accusations. They accused Him of lying, and He replied that He simply spoke what His Father sent Him to speak. When they asked Him where His Father was, He simply told them that they did not know His Father.

The Pharisees continued to accuse Him of lying, saying that He must have a demon inside Him. This confrontation came to a head when Jesus said that Abraham rejoiced to see His day—that is, His arrival. The religious leaders shot back by saying that Jesus wasn't even fifty years old. How could He possibly have known Abraham centuries before?

Jesus replied, "Truly, truly, I say to you, before Abraham was . . . *I AM.*" He deliberately and clearly claimed the unspeakable name of *Yahweh* for Himself (v. 58). He *is* the eternal God that spoke with Abraham. No wonder the religious leaders wanted to stone Him (v. 59).

But Christ spoke the truth. All people must either accept His deity or reject His message. This is why we study the pre-existence and eternality of Christ in this lesson.

. . . .

Student Work

All Christians will meditate on Christ to some degree. After all, God first saved us through the knowledge of His Son. But to grow in Christ, we should carefully and deliberately think on His character and work.

As John Owen wrote, "If our minds are not filled with these things—if Christ doth not dwell plentifully in our hearts by faith—if our souls are not possessed with them . . . we are strangers unto the life of faith."

Why will we think about Christ often? Because we love Him. And why do we love Him? Because of two primary things:

- **Who He Is**—His character, His being, His likeness
- **What He's Done**—His ministry, His sacrifice

Perhaps we are first attracted to Christ by what He did for us. It's in His death and resurrection that we first see His love. But as we grow closer to Him, we begin to love Him not only for His work, but also for His character. We learn to adore Him for who He is. We study His work to cherish His person.

Read Philippians 2:5–11; 3:8–11.

✎ In 2:5–11, did Paul write about God's work or God's Person?

_____

✎ And in 3:8–11, to what is Paul attracted? _____

We worship God for His mighty deeds, but beyond that, we seek to know the One behind it all. We seek the purpose behind the act, the intent behind the work.

Christ's Deity

Many so-called Christian scholars deny the deity of Christ. They claim that we do not need to believe that He was God in order to trust His teaching or

His sacrifice. These same scholars usually deny the pre-existence of Christ, which is strong evidence for His identity as God. If Christ pre-existed His birth, it makes no sense to say that He was only human.

A few lines of reasoning try to subvert this doctrine, including the following two arguments:

1. **Jesus is the Son of God. Therefore, He must have a beginning.**

This argument goes something like the following:

> **Premise A:** Jesus is the Son of God.
> **Premise B:** All sons have a beginning.

> **Conclusion:** Jesus has a beginning.

And further:

> **Premise A:** Jesus has a beginning.
> **Premise B:** God is eternal—He has no beginning.

> **Conclusion:** Jesus is not God.

Can you spot where the argument goes wrong? It assumes a faulty definition of the "Son of God." Jesus was not God's Son in an earthly, biological sense. He had no heavenly mother and no spiritual birth. He—like the "sons" of the prophets in the Old Testament (2 Kings 2:3)—was *of the order* of God. Jesus *proceeded* from God because He was actually God Himself.

In John 1, we learn that Christ, the Word, was with God and also God Himself. Write John 1:3 below:

_____

_____

_____

In your own words, summarize what Colossians 1:15–17 says about Christ.

_____

_____

_____

_____

If we accept Scripture as true, we cannot reasonably question Christ's position as Creator-God. He was never created, but rather created all things.

2. He was only a thought in God's mind.

Another, perhaps more vague argument is that Christ existed before His birth, but only as an idea in God's mind. But Scripture outlines no such doctrine, and it's difficult to accept that an "idea" created the universe.

✐ How else might you address this argument?

_____

_____

_____

_____

_____

Christ's Eternality

Seen in Prophecy

✐ In Micah 5:2, we read one of the most famous prophecies concerning the birth of Christ (cf. Matt. 2:5–6). Where does the prophet record that the Messiah would be born? _____

✐ But the end of the verse claims that this Ruler has existed since . . .

_____

Seen in His Own Words

✐ How does Christ state His eternality in John 17:5?

_____

_____

✐ And again, what name did God reveal to Moses in Exodus 3:14? _____

✐ And what name did Jesus claim in John 8:58? _____

The religious leaders sought to kill Jesus because they would not tolerate His claim of eternality and deity. To deny that Christ is God, therefore, is to stand against Him at His trial and call Him a liar—to actually testify that He deserved to die.

Notes from the Teacher's Lesson

His Pre-Existence Defined

- Christ's pre-existence refers to . . .

  _____

  _____

  _____

  _____

  _____

His Pre-Existence Stated

- _____

- _____

  "Before Abraham was, *I AM*."

The Significance of His Pre-Existence

- The truth of His pre-existence (1 John 5:11–12)

  Our life in Christ is eternal, just as His life is eternal.

- The form of His pre-existence (John 1:1–4)

  - He was _____ (v. 1–2).

  - He was _____ (v. 1).

  - All things were _____ (v. 3).

  - He is the _____ (v. 4).

Application Activities

1. Construct a dialog from John 8, writing down each statement by Christ and His detractors. Write a brief summary of the different peoples' responses to His teaching.

2. Using at least two sources, research one argument against the deity of Christ. In three paragraphs or less, address the argument with both Scripture and logic.

3. Make a list of at least five Scripture passages that state or imply the pre-existence of Christ. Write a brief summary of each.

4. Research two religious groups that deny the deity or pre-existence of Christ.

   - For each group, write one paragraph explaining why they deny this doctrine. Cite at least two reputable sources.

   - Finally, write a third paragraph addressing their arguments.

   Note: your teacher might help you identify reputable sources.

CHAPTER 23

The Incarnation of Christ

"Upon our fall from God, our nature became odious to Him. . . . Christ taking our flesh, makes this human nature appear lovely to God."

—Thomas Watson, *A Body of Divinity*

When most people think about the incarnation of Christ, they think of Christmas. If they can get past all the glitter and gifts and excess that can distract from the meaning of the holiday, they might focus on the story of a tiny baby born in a stable in Bethlehem. They'll appreciate their time with family and friends, and they'll rightly thank God for the gift that is His Son.

But the doctrine of the incarnation runs deeper than that. It's an extraordinarily complex line of thought that makes us wonder at the work and intent of God. How could Christ take on human flesh? How did His humanity serve the purpose of God? Why did He condescend to our state and commune with us? And why did He choose to be born to Mary, a betrothed virgin?

Although the mysteries are many, we will study the Scriptures that describe His incarnation with an eye toward understanding His character. Through this study, we may capture some of the wonder felt by Mary as she praised God for choosing her (Luke 1:46–55). We may understand the joy of Joseph, of shepherds, of Simeon the priest, of Anna the prophetess, of the magi, and all those who saw the Messiah in His infancy.

Student Work

Divine Timing

✎ Though it had been a long time since God first promised the Messiah back in Genesis 3:15, Jesus came to Earth exactly when He planned. How is this idea described in Galatians 4:4?

_____

_____

In the course of Paul's argument to the Galatians, he makes this point to show that God saves each of us in His own timing. We become children of God through the work of Christ.

We cannot comprehend the intent behind God's timetable, but history indicates that the world was uniquely ready for Christ's message at this time. A few examples are helpful.

Greek culture had saturated the nations surrounding the Mediterranean, spreading a robust yet flexible language that many people adopted as their second tongue. Prominent schools and philosophers in the centuries before ensured that the Greek vocabulary and syntax could address complex, abstract concepts—like the theology Paul would include in his epistles.

Built on top of this culture was the Roman Empire, which, despite many internal conflicts, had conquered and united much of the Middle East, northern Africa, and even part of Europe. Though often cruel and oppressive, the Empire dampened petty conflicts between tribes and people groups, and brought with it an excellent system of roads. People and ideas could travel farther and easier than perhaps ever before. Historians call the era between 27 BC and 130 AD the *Pax Romana*—in Latin, the Roman Peace.

Bristling under this rule, however, were the Jewish people, who longed for the coming of their Messiah. King Herod had built them a new Temple in Jerusalem, but they looked for One who could successfully restore the throne of David. They had seen their share of false prophets and fake messiahs, but they still waited for a person who would fulfill the Law perfectly.

Divine Placement

✍ God also chose the exact place where Christ would be born—and the exact person to whom He would be born. Note how the prophecies about the Messiah became more specific over time:

- The Messiah would be born of a woman (Gen. 3:15).

- The Messiah—the One who would bless all peoples of the earth— would be born among Abraham's descendants (Gen. 12:1–3).

- The Messiah would be born into the Israelite tribe of _____ —the tribe that would carry the royal line (Gen. 49:9–12).

- The Messiah would be born to a young woman, understood to be a _____ (Isa. 7:14). He would be called *Immanuel*—that is, "God with us."

- The Messiah would be born in the village of _____ (Mic. 5:2).

God exercised His power to reveal Himself to the world in exactly the way He promised.

Divine Miracle

✍ Read Luke 1:26–38. What problem did Mary see in the angel's news (v. 34)?

_____

✍ Whose power did the angel say would make this miracle happen (v. 35)?

_____

It's impossible to say how God accomplished this wonder, but the spiritual mechanics are irrelevant. Mary, an imperfect person and a virgin, would nonetheless give birth to the perfect God of the universe. As discussed before, this would not be *His* beginning, but rather the beginning of His physical ministry on Earth.

✍ What sign did the angel give Mary to show that God could accomplish this work (v. 36)?

_____

✎ Note also the angel's final assurance. Write Luke 1:37 below:

_____

_____

God, the Creator of the universe, chose to usher in His new Creation by coming to Earth in this way. It served as a sign that this Jesus was special, unencumbered by the sinful heritage of the first man and woman.

Unfortunately, this miracle also meant that Jesus would be called illegitimate by unbelievers. People referred to Him as the "son of Mary" (Mark 6:3)—ignoring Joseph because they assumed that Jesus was fathered by another man. In John 8, when Jesus told the people that they were not actually children of God, they shot back, crudely and pointedly, "*We* weren't born out of sexual immorality" (v. 41).

Like many of God's miracles, the virgin birth is a sign appreciated fully only by believers. Unbelievers will find many ways to mock and deride Christ, but we believers can appreciate the power behind His work.

However, we should not make more of this miracle than Scripture does. For example, the Roman Catholic Church teaches the *perpetual virginity* of Mary—that is, she was married to Joseph, but refrained from sexual activity for her entire life. Further, Catholics assert that God gave Mary the grace to never sin at all—a kind of perfection that sex would supposedly defile. This doctrine likely arose from false assumptions that sex is always at least somewhat dirty or shameful, even within a good marriage.

But Scripture clearly teaches that sexual affection can be a wonderful expression of intimacy within a loving marriage (Gen. 2:21–25; Prov. 5:18–23; Song of Sol. 6:2–3). It's not a necessary evil or in any way unholy—it's a fantastic way for a husband and wife to celebrate each other as one flesh. Of course, we can express our sexuality in harmful, sinful ways, but that's not what God originally intended.

Mary and Joseph put off sexual intimacy for a time—Matthew 1:25 says that they did not *ginosko* ("know") each other until after Jesus was born. However, we read in Mark 6:3 and elsewhere that Jesus had a number of brothers and sisters, including James, Joses, Judas, and Simon. Roman Catholics explain these away as children from Joseph's previous marriage, but Scripture indicates no such thing.

In short, believers shouldn't deny the virgin birth of Christ, but they also shouldn't build doctrine around the miracle that Scripture doesn't support. Such doctrines are not only untrue, but also distracting from the point. We marvel at the virgin birth because we marvel at *Immanuel*—God is *with* us!

Divine Praise

✒ Read Luke 1:46–56. Who praised the Lord in this passage (v. 46)?

_____

✒ This passage is often called the *Magnificat*. List the attributes of God referenced in this song.

_____

_____

_____

_____

_____

Note three key elements of Mary's praise:

Magnification *(v. 46)*

Mary magnified the Lord. With her praise, she made God seem *near*. He is close and comforting to those who trust Him.

Like Mary, we should help others see God as a very real and present power in their lives. We can magnify God through our praise and through our obedience.

Rejoicing *(v. 47–49)*

We find joy in God. This does not come from a temporary, bubbling happiness. This is a deep, abiding knowledge of the grace and hope we have in Christ. This kind of joy takes time to prepare and strengthen, but it helps us long after feelings of elation pass.

Over time, however, the joy will affect the way we feel. When God works in an incredible way—as He did with Mary—our hearts can resonate with His love, and we will overflow with wonder at His goodness.

✎ Look at verses 48 and 49 again, and write the phrase that best reflects each of the following statements.

- Mary was lowly and imperfect.

  _____

  _____

- Mary would be a symbol of God's grace for all time.

  _____

  _____

- This miracle was the work of her mighty God.

  _____

  _____

Remembrance *(vv. 50–55)*

Mary's praise also reflected the work of God in the past. God certainly chose her for a special role, but His goodness and power toward her was not new or unique. He had always helped His people, and Jesus would serve as the fulfillment of God's promises.

Like Mary, we have truly been blessed of God by Christ. We, too, can trust in the work of our Savior, and we, too, can know the Son of God.

Notes from the Teacher's Lesson

The Doctrine of Christ

His History	His Offices	His Person	His Names
• His pre-existence	• Prophet	• His deity	• Jesus
• His incarnation and virgin birth	• Priest	• His humanity	• Christ
• His sinless life	• King		• Lord of Glory
• His death			. . . and others
• His resurrection			
• His ascension and exaltation			

Christ's Incarnation Defined

- Within Christianity, the *incarnation* refers to . . .

  _____

His Incarnation Stated

- _____

- *Theophanies* are . . .

  _____

  _____

The Significance of His Incarnation

- He chose to _____ (Heb. 4:14–15).
- He chose to _____ (Heb. 1:3–4).
  - He revealed God's _____ (John 1:14–17).
  - He revealed God's _____.

. . . .

Application Activities

1. Research the Roman Catholic position on the perfection of Mary, and write three paragraphs summarizing the doctrine you find. Cite at least two reputable sources. Note: your teacher might help you identify reputable sources.

2. Write two paragraphs explaining what you believe is the meaning behind Luke 2:52. In what way did Christ choose to develop? Outline your own thoughts before you consult other writers, and cite any sources you use.

3. Read Chapter 4 ("The Glory of Christ's Humbling Himself") in John Owen's book *The Glory of Christ*. List and summarize what you learn from your reading.

CHAPTER 24

The Impeccability and Atonement of Christ

"A great many people are trying to make peace, but that has already been done. God has not left it for us to do; all we have to do is enter into it."

—D. L. Moody, *The New Book of Christian Quotations*

In 1875, Fanny Crosby published the poem, "To God Be the Glory," which would become one of her most famous hymns:

> To God be the glory, great things He hath done,
> So loved He the world that He gave us His Son,
> Who yielded His life an atonement for sin,
> And opened the life gate that all may go in.
>
> Oh, perfect redemption, the purchase of blood,
> To every believer the promise of God;
> The vilest offender who truly believes,
> That moment from Jesus a pardon receives.
>
> Great things He hath taught us, great things He hath done,
> And great our rejoicing through Jesus the Son;
> But purer, and higher, and greater will be
> Our wonder, our transport, when Jesus we see.

Refrain:

> Praise the Lord, praise the Lord, let the earth hear His voice!
> Praise the Lord, praise the Lord, let the people rejoice!
>
> Oh, come to the Father through Jesus the Son,
> And give Him the glory, great things He hath done.

In these lyrics, Crosby captured the essence of the gospel. God revealed His glory through the life, death, and resurrection of Christ. By His sacrifice, God purchased our redemption. In the blood of Christ we see a symbol of the life He gave up for us—then claimed again by conquering death and sin.

We stand in horror at the suffering Christ endured because of our sin, yet we also find joy. Because He redeemed us, we can know Him, praise Him, and one day live with Him forever.

. . . .

Student Work

His Impeccability

Jesus Christ is the only person to have lived perfectly without sin. All others have fallen short of God's glory (Rom. 3:23), including the prominent men and women that God used in the Bible.

Read the following verses, and write what each person said about their own sin.

- Isaiah 6:5—Isaiah exclaimed,

  _____

  _____

- Psalm 51:3—David cried,

  _____

  _____

- 1 Timothy 1:15—Paul wrote,

  _____

  _____

Jesus, however, never expressed guilt or remorse. He never asked the Father to forgive Him, and He never gave His disciples a personal example of repentance. But He did instruct others to turn from their sin. Whenever He asked the Father to forgive—such as He did on the cross (Luke 23:34)—He made the request on behalf of others.

Christ's sinlessness is a major part of the gospel because God's Law required a perfect sacrifice.

For each of the following passages, summarize the phrase that best indicates the impeccability of Jesus.

✎ The Testimony of the Apostles

- 1 John 3:5

  _____

- 1 Peter 2:22

  _____

  _____

- 2 Corinthians 5:21

  _____

- Hebrews 4:15

  _____

  _____

- Acts 3:14

  _____

  _____

✎ The Testimony of Christ Himself

- John 8:46

  _____

  _____

- John 14:30–31

  _____

  _____

  _____

Even Christ's enemies recognized His blamelessness. Pilate and his wife could not say that He had done anything wrong (Matt. 27:19, 24), and the demons called Him the "Holy One of God" (Mark 1:24).

As discussed earlier, this holiness was not merely the absence of sin. Jesus was perfect and exalted, exactly like the Father and the Spirit.

The Atonement

✎ In Galatians 2:20 we see the grace of the gospel. Write the verse below:

_____

_____

_____

_____

_____

Christ gave Himself for us, and we cannot yet fathom the full reason why. We cannot yet understand the height or depth of His love.

✎ After Paul wrote about the mysteries of the gospel in Romans 11, how did he describe the mind of God (vv. 33–36)?

_____

_____

_____

_____

We could not address every doctrine concerning atonement in a few pages, but we will explore the following points.

The Nature of His Atonement

Read each of the passages below, then write the reference under the doctrinal heading it best describes. Write each reference only once.

- Isaiah 53:6
- John 10:17–18
- Acts 2:23
- 2 Corinthians 5:21
- 1 Peter 2:24
- 1 Peter 3:18

Christ's Atonement Was Substitutionary

✎ *Scripture:* _____

_____

Christ gave His life as a substitution for the life that we should have given. He died in our place, He bore our sins, and He suffered the punishment that we deserved. This was not a vain martyrdom. Since Christ died for us, we no longer need to die. God's justice is satisfied, and He will not direct His wrath toward those who trust in Christ.

Christ's Atonement Was Volitional

✎ *Scripture:* _____

Christ suffered voluntarily. He was not forced, coerced, or tricked into dying for us. He came to Earth knowing that He would die, and He chose to face this task out of love for us.

Christ's Atonement Was Predetermined

✎ *Scripture:* _____

Again, Christ's death was no accident. It was part of God's plan from the very beginning, long before He created the world. Christ's enemies may have felt a sense of victory when they saw Him on the cross, but they were actually tools of His sovereignty. God orchestrated even the death of Christ to accomplish His own glorious plan.

The Results of His Atonement

What did Christ accomplish through the atonement? If we accept Him, what does His work mean for us?

As you did in the previous exercise, read each passage and write the reference under the appropriate doctrine. This time, some passages may fall under multiple headings.

- Matthew 5:17
- Matthew 26:28
- John 12:31–32
- Romans 5:9
- Romans 5:10
- Romans 8:19–23

- Galatians 3:13
- Ephesians 1:7
- Colossians 1:20
- 1 Timothy 2:6
- Hebrews 2:14–15
- Hebrews 9:15

- Hebrews 10:10
- Hebrews 10:19–22
- 1 Peter 1:18–19
- 2 Peter 3:13
- 1 John 2:2
- 1 John 4:10

Christ Met the Requirements of the Law

✎ *Scripture:* _____

Christ obeyed the spirit and letter of the Old Testament Law perfectly. He became the perfect sacrifice that all the rituals of the Law symbolized and predicted. He is the Messiah to which all the Law and the prophets pointed.

Christ Defeated Satan

✏ *Scripture:* _____

By His death and resurrection, Christ sealed the fate of the Enemy. If Satan thought that he had any speck of power against the God of the universe, any such notion fled at the sight of the empty tomb. Satan's punishment is as sure as our redemption.

Christ Offered Us Forgiveness

✏ *Scripture:* _____

Christ's death paid for our sin. He *remitted* our sins—that is, He canceled our debt by paying it off Himself. Our sins no longer blot our record before God.

Christ's sacrifice was the means by which a just God would forgive sinful people like us. God would not overlook even the slightest sin, so to establish perfect justice, He took on Himself the punishment for our sin, thereby offering us a way to receive His forgiveness.

Christ Removed the Fear of Death

✏ *Scripture:* _____

The sting of death is gone, and we need never fear it. Beyond physical death lies eternal life, and we can trust that our departure from this world will precede an arrival at God's glorious home.

Christ Redeemed Us to God

✏ *Scripture:* _____

_____

Christ bought us back by paying the penalty for our sin. We were once slaves to sin, but now we are children of God.

Christ Justified Us Before God

✐ *Scripture:* _____

Through Christ, God declares us innocent and righteous. God not only forgives our sins, but also accepts us as if we had never sinned in the first place. When God looks at us, He sees the perfection of Christ. As believers, we can still sin, but that will affect our *walk* with God, our core *relationship* with Him.

Christ Reconciled Us to God

✐ *Scripture:* _____
_____

Christ made peace between us and God. Our sin turned us away from the Father, but Christ turned us back toward Him.

Christ was our *propitiation*—that is, He satisfied God's justice. Because of Christ's sacrifice, we need never fear God's anger.

Christ Sanctified Us to God

✐ *Scripture:* _____

Christ set us apart from sin for a particular purpose—to glorify Him. And the Spirit continues to sanctify us, making us more holy as we abide in God. One day, beyond eternity, we will be perfect reflections of God's character.

Christ Gave Us Communion with God

✐ *Scripture:* _____

Through Christ our High Priest, we have access to God. We can learn His truth in the Word; we can talk with Him through prayer; and we can see His hand in the world around us. No one should or could stand between us and our Father. We can go directly to Him, knowing that He hears us, cares for us, and will work toward our good.

Christ Made Us Heirs of God

✐ Scripture: _____

As God's children, we are heirs to all the riches of His grace. We can live in His joy, peace, and love now, and we have also the sure hope of an inheritance with Him in heaven.

Christ Redeemed the Universe

✐ Scripture: _____

All of Creation was cursed because of humanity's sin. It therefore declines toward chaos and death. But one day, God will restore or recreate all of this, making it incorruptibly perfect for all eternity. Christ began that redemption at the cross.

As you've probably realized, the atonement was an incredibly complex work of Christ. No one picture can fully capture its meaning. As long as we study the Word, we will find new levels and new intricacies to our salvation.

Notes from the Teacher's Lesson

Christ's Impeccability

- The definition of impeccability:

  ○ _____

  ○ _____

- The statement of His impeccability:

  ○ _____

  ○ _____

- The significance of His impeccability:

  ○ It marks _____ (John 8:46; 1 John 1:8–10).

  ○ It empowers the _____ (1 Pet. 1:18–19).

  ○ It enables _____ (Heb. 4:15–16).

  ○ It demands _____ from us.

The Atonement of Christ

- The definition of atonement:

  ○ *Atonement*

    _____

    _____

  ○ *Reconciliation*

    _____

    _____

  ○ *Propitiation*

    _____

    _____

- The statement of His atonement:

  ○ _____

  ○ _____

- The significance of His atonement:

  ○ _____—His death satisfies God.

  ○ _____—His death restores us to God (Eph. 2:11–22).

Application Activities

1. In a one-page paper, describe one or two sacrifices or festivals prescribed by Old Testament Law, and compare each sacrifice or festival with the sacrifice of Christ on the cross.

2. Read Chapter 3 ("The Sacrifice of Isaac") and Chapter 10 ("The Passover Lamb") of Robert T. Ketcham's book, *Old Testament Pictures of New Testament Truth*. List and summarize what you learn from your reading.

3. List at least ten songs or hymns that address the doctrine of the atonement. Choose three of them, and write a paragraph for each, summarizing what they teach about the meaning of Christ's death.

CHAPTER 25

The Resurrection of Christ

"Christ's rising is a pledge of our resurrection. . . . As the first-fruits is a sure evidence that the harvest is coming, so the resurrection of Christ is a sure evidence of the rising of our bodies from the grave."

—Thomas Watson, *A Body of Divinity*

Near the end of World War II, when U.S. General Dwight Eisenhower first discovered the conditions of prisoners in German concentration camps, he immediately ordered the U.S. Army Signal Corps to photograph and film the survivors and the dead. In addition, Eisenhower personally visited camps when they were liberated—as many as his duties would allow. He also asked the U.S. and British governments to quickly send a contingent of journalists and historians to document the camps, though not many people could stand to witness these horrors for long.

Why did Eisenhower do this? Because, he said later, "in case there ever grew up at home the belief or assumption that the stories of Nazi brutality were just propaganda." Nearly every government in the war—including the United States—had relied on propaganda to motivate its citizens, but Eisenhower did not want the horrors of the Holocaust dismissed as such a lie.

Unfortunately, Eisenhower's concerns were well-founded. Throughout the world today, groups find it convenient to deny the fact that the Nazis murdered six million Jews and another five million "undesirables." In an attempt to justify their anti-Semitism, these groups call the Holocaust a Jewish conspiracy—despite innumerable photographs, films, and eyewitness accounts to the contrary.

Unless the Spirit works in people's hearts, they will believe what they want to believe. For example, we cannot *force* people to believe that Christ rose from the dead—this must be accepted by faith. Even if we could prove it beyond all doubt, many people would still deny it and turn from God. We know this because the chief priests and Pharisees, despite all evidence, refused to accept the resurrection of Jesus.

We can, however, demonstrate that the resurrection is reasonable and consistent with the truth of Scripture—and further, that on this doctrine depends the certainty of our hope in God.

Student Work

Confirming the Resurrection

The New Testament writers took great pains to emphasize the literal resurrection of Christ. By carefully including physical details and the accounts of numerous eyewitnesses, they ruled out any future claims that Christ merely disappeared or arose in some vague, spiritual way. To deny the resurrection of Christ, therefore, is to deny the accuracy and inspiration of Scripture.

The following are a some examples of these details:

The Moved Stone

The tombs of wealthy individuals in the time of Christ were chiseled out of rocky cliffs, often facing a small garden. Jesus did not purchase such a tomb for Himself, but a wealthy man, Joseph of Arimathea, donated his own prepared tomb when Christ died.

Tombs such as this featured a trench running in front of the doorway. A disc-shaped stone would be rolled down the inclined trench to seal the tomb. Easy to close but difficult to open, the tomb would thus be safe from all but the most determined grave robbers.

As described in Matthew 27, Pilate ordered that Christ's tomb be sealed after the burial—in part to placate those religious leaders who thought that the disciples might try to steal the body and claim Jesus' resurrection. The stone cover already required a group of people to move, and the extra seal made it almost impossible. The Romans had developed an early form of concrete, and they likely fitted this around the tomb's doorway. They may also have fastened a cord in front of the stone, stamped on each side by a clay seal, a mark that would be illegal for anyone to remove. On top of that, Pilate posted a guard of soldiers in the garden.

✎ We can therefore understand why Mary Magdalene, Salome, and the other Mary wondered how they might reach Christ's body to anoint Him (Mark 16:1–3). But according to Luke 24:2, where did the women find the stone?

_____

If this stone was as large as others found by archeologists in the area, it may have weighed more than a ton (900 kg). If so, who moved it?

✎ Read Matthew 27:62–66. Would the soldiers or the enemies of Christ have any motivation to roll away the stone and make His body disappear? Why or why not?

_____
_____
_____
_____
_____
_____

To steal Christ's body, the disciples would need to overpower a group of soldiers, break the seal on the stone, and pull it out of place. Yet according to Scripture, the guards reported no such thing.

The Empty Tomb

Read Matthew 28:5–6 and John 20:3–10. As discussed in the teacher's lesson, some people have tried to explain away this part of Scripture by proposing alternative reasons for the body's disappearance. Uncomfortable with the idea of resurrection, they invent theories that justify their view of Christ as a good—yet very much dead—man.

The Wrong-Tomb Theory

This theory proposes that the women stumbled into the wrong tomb that morning. Their visions of the angel and Christ must have been shared delusions.

The Swoon Theory

As discussed in the teacher's lesson, some people speculate that Christ somehow survived the horrors of the cross, was stabbed with a spear, was taken down from the cross, and was buried by people who mistook Him for dead. Then He lay for a few days in a cold tomb, after which, despite the lack of medical care, water, or food, He somehow forced open the seal and stumbled out into the garden, whereupon He snuck past the guards, who evidently didn't notice the tomb cracking open.

It's difficult to imagine how a human could do this. Why not simply deny the Scriptures outright? Likewise, if you accept that Jesus is God, why not trust that He rose again, as He promised?

The Stolen-Body Theory

✎ Read Matthew 28:11–15. How did the enemies of Christ try to spread doubt about His resurrection?

_____

_____

_____

_____

✎ Why might this lie seem implausible?

_____

_____

_____

_____

_____

_____

_____

Some people will reject God's truth even if they can't offer a good reason.

✐ As Christ revealed in the story of Lazarus and the rich man, what did Abraham say about those who reject God (Luke 16:31)?

_____

_____

_____

_____

The Grave Clothes

✐ According to John 20:6–7, the tomb was not *quite* empty. When the disciples looked inside, what did they see?

_____

_____

_____

_____

Scripture indicates that Christ's body was prepared in the traditional manner (Matt. 27:57–61), which means He was likely wrapped in linen bands that enclosed a large amount of perfumed spices. One such spice, Aloes, was a wood that, when powdered, emitted a strong fragrance. Myrrh—an edible, aromatic tree resin—could be mixed in, as well.

The linen shroud covering the body could enclose nearly 100 pounds (45 kg) of spices, as well. The cloth would reach from the feet to the upper chest, leaving the shoulders, neck, and face of the body bare. A separate cloth wrapped around the top of the head like a turban.

When the disciples looked into the tomb, they saw the cloths lying there in their separate places, almost as if the body had simply disappeared from within them. If people had stolen the body, it seems doubtful that they would have left all of these articles undisturbed.

The Soldiers

✍ Read Matthew 28:1–4. Describe what frightened the soldiers that morning.

_____

_____

_____

_____

_____

This is what the soldiers reported to the chief priests, whom Pilate authorized to oversee the guard. But after consulting together, the religious leaders bribed the guards into spreading the rumor that the disciples had somehow stolen the body.

Scripture would not include this account if the literal resurrection was not important.

The Appearances of Christ

✍ Scripture reveals at least eleven appearances of Christ after His resurrection and before His ascension to heaven. Read the following passages, and write who saw Jesus in each instance.

- John 20:11–17—_____

- Luke 24:34; 1 Corinthians 15:5—_____,
  also known as Peter

- Mark 16:12–13; Luke 24:13–35—_____

- Luke 24:36–43; John 20:19–23—_____

  ○ How did He show them He was not a spirit?

  _____

  _____

- John 20:26–29—_____

- 1 Corinthians 15:6—_____

Living the Resurrection

Some Christians seem satisfied enough that Jesus died, but they place no importance on His resurrection. But Mary and the other believers had no such attitude. For Christ's teaching and promises to be true, He needed to *live*. His resurrection filled His followers with joy because in that act He demonstrated the power needed to establish His eternal kingdom. Jesus is not a Savior we remember fondly—we walk with Him *today*, and we trust Him to secure all the ages to come.

Note the difference in Christ's disciples before and after they knew of His resurrection. At first they hid in fear (John 20:19), but later they shared the gospel far beyond Jerusalem and Israel. Peter denied Jesus thrice before the crucifixion, but later, at Pentecost, the disciple spoke boldly to thousands.

Paul described the importance of the resurrection in 1 Corinthians 15:14–19. For each verse listed below, write what must be true if Christ did not rise from the dead.

- Verse 14—_____
- Verse 15—_____
  _____
- Verse 17—_____
  _____
- Verse 18—_____
  _____
- Verse 19—_____

Upon this good news we build all our faith and hope. Without a living Savior, we deserve only pity. The resurrection is the difference between a lifeless religion and a living relationship.

How has the good news of Christ changed you? Do you allow this joy to infuse your thoughts, words, and actions? Do you share the gospel? Do you think of Christ as some distant historical figure, or do you know Him as your Savior, Sustainer, and Friend? Do you merely study the good He did, or do you reflect that same grace in your life?

Notes from the Teacher's Lesson

The Resurrection Defined

- The correct definition:

  _____

  _____

  _____

  _____

- Two false definitions:

  ○ The _____ Theory – Christ, although not literally risen from the dead, still lives in the hearts and minds of His followers.

  ○ The _____ Theory – Christ arose in some spiritual form—He enjoyed continued existence after His death—but not in a physical, bodily form.

Christ's Resurrection Stated

- The account in all four Gospels:

  ○ _____   ○ _____

  ○ _____   ○ _____

- Luke's summary of the forty days after the resurrection:

  _____

- Paul's resurrection chapter:

  _____

The Nature of Christ's Resurrection

- He arose _____.

  ○ The _____ in His hands and feet (Ps. 22:16; Zech. 12:10; John 20:25–29)

  ○ The _____ in His side (John 20:25–29)

- o The _____ of His disciples

- o The _____ He ate (Luke 24:41–43)

- o The tactility of His body

    - Mary Magdalene and the other Mary held Him outside the tomb (Matt. 28:9).

    - He invited the disciples to touch Him (Luke 24:33–43).

    - John assured people that Christ was alive by writing that he touched Jesus with his own hands (1 John 1:1).

- He arose _____ (Eph. 1:15–21).

The Significance of Christ's Resurrection *(1 Cor. 15:14–19)*

- The _____ of Christ (Rom. 1:1–4)

- The _____ of Scripture

- Our _____ (Rom. 4:24–25)

- Our _____ (Rom. 6:4)

- Our _____ (John 14:3; 1 Thess. 4:14; Phil. 1:23)

- The _____ (Acts 17:30–31)

- The future _____ (1 Cor. 15:20–23, 52–57)

Application Activities

1. Research one so-called relic of Christ's death and resurrection. In one page or less, answer the following questions, and cite any sources you use.

    -   What connection does this object supposedly have with Christ?

    -   Who makes this claim?

    -   In your opinion, what is the credibility of this claim?

    -   Are there similar or duplicate objects that make conflicting claims?

2. Read Matthew 28 carefully, asking God to show you His character and work. List all of the things you see about God in that chapter, and include your thoughts about Him as our Savior.

3. Using any category, record a providence in which the truth of Christ's resurrection was important.

4. Research the origins of the Easter holiday.

    -   In one page or less, describe its roots in both Christian and non-Christian traditions. Cite any sources you use.

    -   If you were asked to come up with a new, explicitly Christian name for the holiday, what would you choose?

5. Research the locations that people claim may be the site of Christ's tomb.

    -   For each location you find, write a paragraph summarizing its ownership and history. Cite any sources you use, and include relevant photographs in your paper, if possible.

    -   In a concluding paragraph, state which location you believe has the best historical claim, and why.

CHAPTER 26

The Ascension of Christ

"In His resurrection He was exalted above the grave, in His ascension He was exalted above the starry and airy heavens, in His sitting at God's right hand He was exalted far above the highest heavens."

—Thomas Watson, *A Body of Divinity*

Throughout history, kingdoms and empires have bestowed on their rulers symbols of power and authority. A crown, a scepter, a throne—these objects do not *give* authority, but they do *represent* it.

- **The Uraeus**—an upright cobra that adorned the headdress of Egyptian pharaohs. This symbolized the approval of the goddess Wadjet, the serpent associated with the Milky Way in the night sky. God seemed to take special care to tarnish this symbol when He sent Moses back into Egypt.

- **The Persian Scepter**—a long, lightly adorned rod shown in reliefs of ancient Persian rulers. The scepter of King Ahasuerus marked a key moment in the story of Esther (8:4), when she approached his throne despite not having been summoned.

- **The Toga Picta**—the "painted toga," worn by Roman generals at a ceremony celebrating their victories in foreign wars. Featuring an off-white linen with a wide purple border, this garment was initially worn only on special occasions by heroes of the Republic. Over time, however, the Caesars of the Empire wore the toga picta in public as a symbol of strength—much like tyrants who wear excessive military regalia today.

- **The Heirloom Seal of the Realm**—a piece of jade that bore the mark of the Qin Dynasty in China. The seal served emperors and empresses into the Tang Dynasty, but was lost or destroyed sometime after AD 900.

- **The Stone of Scone** (pronounced *skoon*)—also called the Stone of Destiny, a large block of red sandstone that represents the rule of Scotland. The English King Edward I seized the stone from the Scots in 1296, placing it under the English throne to symbolize his united rule of the isle. Scots would later try to take the stone back, with the most famous attempt on Christmas Day in 1950. Four Scottish students hauled the stone out of Westminster Abbey, breaking it in half on their way back to Scotland. Four months later, British officials found the broken stone on the altar of Arbroath Abbey, though rumors persist that the object they found was actually a copy. Regardless, English royals returned the stone to Scotland in 1996, where it now rests in Edinburgh Castle.

Authorities choose these objects as symbols of strength, unity, and permanence, but history teaches us that all human empires eventually weaken, fragment, and fail. The Kingdom of Christ, however, will never end. When Christ ascended into heaven and sat exalted at the right hand of the Father, His marks of authority shone with the same brightness and truth that we will see for all of eternity.

Christ did not gain new power at the exaltation, but God chose this time to make His pre-eminence absolutely clear. We therefore study the ascension and exaltation of Christ to emphasize His finished work and His eternal sovereignty.

Student Work

The Marks of Christ's Exaltation

Exaltation by Title and Office

✐ Read Philippians 2:8–11. Because Christ humbled Himself to die on the cross, what has God given Him (v. 9)?

_____

_____

✐ Describe the kind of respect that this will one day command (vv. 10–11).

_____

_____

_____

_____

Christ is not merely our Savior—He is our Lord, our Ruler, our King. As He taught His disciples on many occasions, to follow Him is to serve Him. We must reflect His truth and love, and we must submit our will to His plan.

✐ Read Acts 5:30–31. What two things is Christ called here (v. 31)?

_____

✐ And what does Christ do in these roles (v. 31)?

_____

_____

✐ Christ alone can offer this to sinners like us. Write Acts 4:12 below.

_____

_____

_____

_____

_____

As we'll study in the following lesson, Christ now fulfills His duties toward us as Prophet, Priest, and King.

Exaltation by Ascension

The Scriptures tie the ascension and the exaltation so closely together that it's fair to say they may be the same event. It's almost as if, when Christ rose from the Mount of Olives, He didn't stop rising until He appeared at the right hand of the Father in heaven. The ascension, therefore, is properly understood as another mark of His exaltation—that is, another representation of His authority.

✎ Read Luke 24:50–53, noting also Acts 1:6–11. To the disciples, this must have been a spectacularly dramatic event. How did they respond to all of this (Luke 24:52–53)?

_____

_____

_____

_____

_____

While much of Christ's earthly ministry demonstrated great humility, this moment marked His rightful assumption of all the glory and power He deserved. Note a brief, incomplete comparison:

Christ on Earth	Christ in Heaven
He was born in a stable and lay in a manger.	He ascended to sit on a throne.
He was despised.	He is worshipped continually.
He was crowned with thorns.	He is crowned with glory.
His robes were torn and gambled away.	He is clothed in light and gold.
He was forsaken by the Father.	He sits in honor at the Father's right hand.

Read Revelation 1:12–20 to see how John struggled to describe Christ's present form. Summarize each element from the description below:

- His clothing—_____
  _____

- His hair—_____

- His eyes—_____

- His feet—_____

- His voice—_____

- His right hand—_____

- His mouth—_____
  _____

- His face—_____

✎ Given the text of John 1 and Hebrews 4:12, what do you think is the meaning behind the image proceeding from Christ's mouth?

_____
_____
_____
_____
_____
_____

In Christ's appearance we see all the might and goodness of the universe. This majesty lay behind the humble carpenter's son in Galilee, but is now perfectly revealed in heaven. We will one day witness His glory for ourselves.

Notes from the Teacher's Lesson

The Ascension of Christ Defined

_____

_____

_____

The Ascension of Christ Stated

- The ascension described (Luke 24:50–53; Acts 1:6–12):

    ○ It occurred with the _____.

    ○ It occurred on the _____, near Bethany.

    ○ It mirrored the _____ (Zech. 14:4–7).

- The ascension predicted:

    _____

- The ascension referenced:

    ○ Romans 8:34

    ○ Colossians 3:1

    ○ Hebrews 1:3; 4:14; 6:20; 8:1; 9:12, 24; 10:12; 12:2; and 13:20

    ○ 1 Timothy 3:16

    ○ 1 Peter 3:22

The Significance of the Ascension

- The significance to Christ:

    ○ It marked the _____ of His earthly work (Heb. 10:12).

    ○ It marked His exaltation (Eph. 1:20–23; Phil. 2:9–11).

Exaltation

_____

_____

_____

○ It began His heavenly _____ (Heb. 4:14–16).

• The significance to believers:

○ It emphasized _____.

○ It assures us of _____.

○ It preceded the _____
of the Holy Spirit (John 16:7).

○ It assures us of our _____
(John 14:1–3).

Application Activities

1. Read Philippians 2:5–11. Record everything you see about Jesus as Savior and Lord.

2. Record a providence in which God answered your prayers in a clear or unusual way.

3. For the next three weeks, record a prayer journal, listing the requests and praises you bring before God each day. Leave room to note how God works through each situation over the next few weeks. Consider maintaining this journal in the weeks and months to come.

4. Find and list at least three distinct passages describing Christ as our Mediator, Advocate, or Intercessor in heaven. For each reference, summarize what the passage states or indicates about how Christ represents us before God today.

5. Read and summarize in writing Chapters 5, 6, and 7 ("The Glory of Christ's Love as Mediator," "The Glory of Christ's Work as Mediator," "The Glory of Christ's Exaltation") in John Owen's book *The Glory of Christ*.

UNIT 5
The Person of Christ

"Christ had a twofold substance, divine and human, yet not a twofold subsistence, both natures make but one Christ. . . . This union of the two natures in Christ was not by transmutation, the divine nature changed into the human, or the human into the divine; nor by mixture, the two natures mingled together . . . but both the natures of Christ remain distinct, and yet make not two distinct persons, but one person; the human nature not God, yet one with God."

—Thomas Watson, *A Body of Divinity*

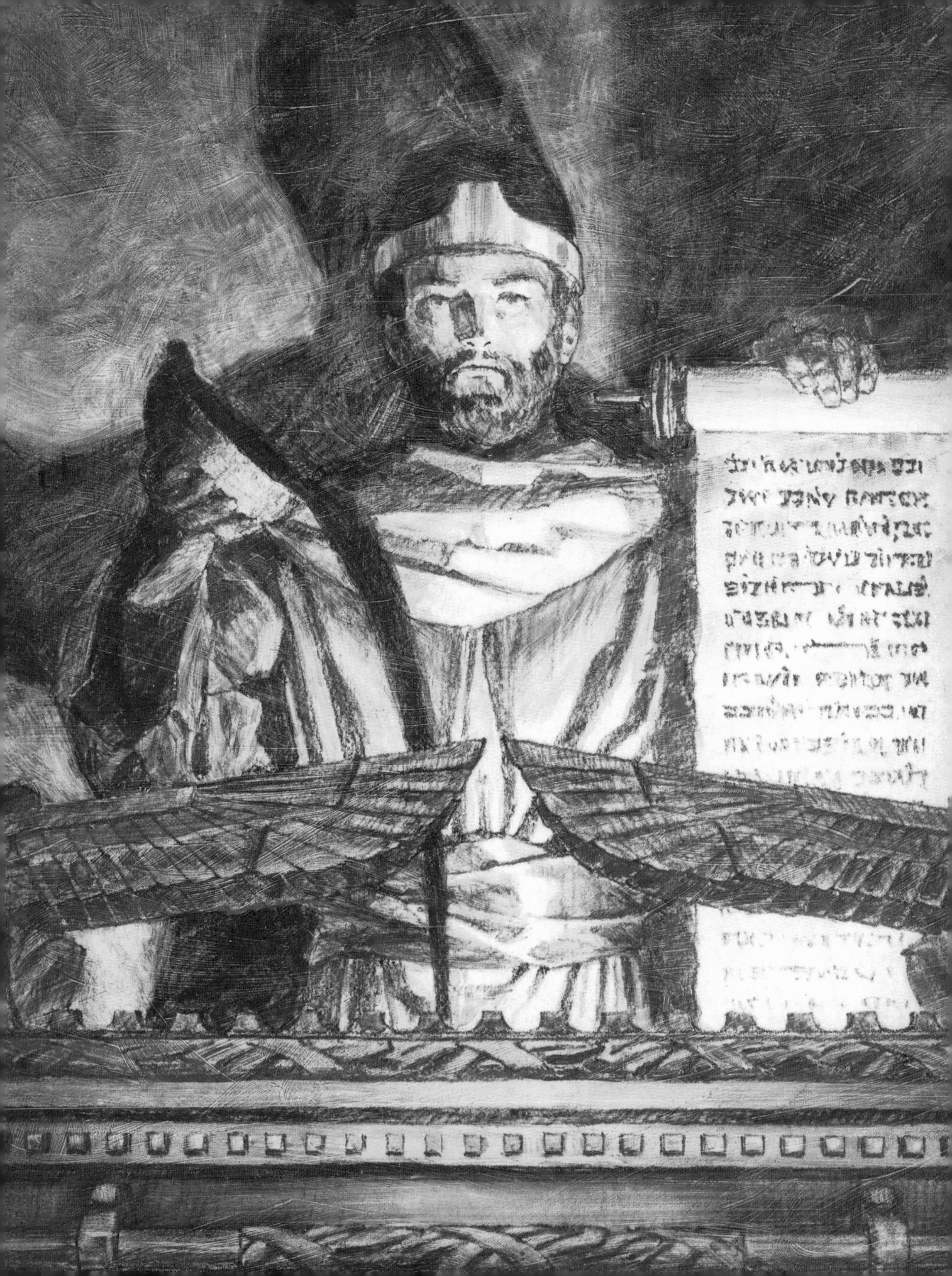

CHAPTER 27

Christ as Prophet, Priest, and King

"Ministers may set the food of the Word before you, and carve it out to you; but it is only Christ can cause you to taste it. . . . [Christ's priestly sacrifice] procures justification of our persons, acceptance of our service, access to God with boldness, and entrance into the holy place of heaven. . . . Christ did not need subjects, He has legions of angels ministering to Him; but in His love He has honored you to make you His subjects."

—Thomas Watson, *A Body of Divinity*

Many jobs, especially those in small businesses, require employees to fulfill more than a single role or responsibility. For example, a small real estate business might hire someone as a real estate agent, with the primary function of selling property to potential buyers. The employee should have the training, experience, and certification necessary to fulfill this role. However, since the business is so small, the employee may also be expected to meet other expectations—filling out paperwork, answering the phone, troubleshooting computer software, or vacuuming the front office.

Social and familial roles involve a variety of responsibilities, as well. Parents and legal guardians are expected to provide a safe, nurturing, and loving environment for children, which may require them to work multiple jobs, maintain a household, cook food, and offer counsel and comfort when needed. Their duties extend above and beyond any full-time career—it becomes a calling that consumes much of what they once considered their own personal time. It takes time, energy, and a great deal of personal sacrifice to protect children, provide for them, and prepare them for their own journey through the world. No parent is perfect—some, in fact, do great harm to their children—but those who do reflect the grace of God deserve great respect.

In the Old Testament, God gave the nation of Israel prophets, priests, and kings. God anointed those individuals to their particular offices, gave them explicit directions on how to discharge their duties, remained with them in the performance of those duties, and accepted their work to the extent they followed His guidance.

Today, however, God has united all of these offices and their various responsibilities in one person—the Lord Jesus Christ. He is the perfect example of servant-leadership and the sole focus of spiritual authority.

In this lesson, we'll examine Christ's role as our Prophet, our Priest, and our King.

. . . .

Student Work

Christ as Our Prophet

When many people hear the word *prophet*, they think of someone who foretells the future. But the foundation of the office is deeper than that. A prophet is a preacher and a teacher of God's truth. That truth can relate to the past, the present, or the future, but it should always relate to God's character and work.

The Old and New Testaments identify a number of people as prophets, including the following:

- Abraham, through whom God revealed His covenant with Israel
- Deborah, who judged the tribes of Israel
- David, whose throne would be renewed by the Messiah
- Isaiah, who prophesied about God's work throughout the ages
- Anna, who recognized the infant Jesus as the Messiah
- The daughters of Philip, who aided Paul's ministry

The Scriptures contain numerous examples of believers who received special truth from God and then shared it with others, thereby assuming the role of prophet. Jesus Christ, however, is the greatest example of truth. As our prophet, He is the Master Teacher. He lived and spoke in perfect truth, as only God Himself could.

Human prophets have no inherent truth or authority—they are wholly dependent on the One who employs them. They present God's truth through the limitations of their own knowledge and personality. Ideally, they are the voice, not the speaker—the instrument, not the artist.

Let's briefly look at Christ's prophetic ministry, which began after His baptism in the Jordan River.

Predictive Truth

✎ Christ foretold numerous events. According to John 13:19 and 14:29, why did He prophesy about future events?

_____

_____

✎ What did Christ predict in the following references?

- Luke 21:20–28—_____

  _____

- Mark 13:2—_____

  _____

- Matthew 24:36–44—_____

  _____

Authoritative Truth

Christ's listeners noted that He did not speak as others did—He spoke as a person who had authority. He knew the Scriptures well, and He taught them with certainty, the kind of certainty that only their Author should have.

✎ Read Mark 12:35–37. According to Jesus, what was the problem with calling the Christ the "Son of David"? Because David called the Messiah (the Christ) his _____.

Christ points this out as an apparent contradiction in Scripture. In Jewish culture, children ascribed authority to their parents, not the other way around. Why then would David ascribe lordship to the Messiah, who would be one of his descendants? It makes no sense, and Jesus noted this impossibility to show the limits of the scribes' understanding.

As the Messiah, however, Jesus knew the answer to this riddle. David called the Messiah Lord because the Messiah was actually God. Yes, Jesus was born into the line of David, but He also *preceded* David as the eternal Lord of all.

Only the Author of Scripture could explain a passage with such familiarity and authority.

Revelatory Truth

✏ Christ is the living revelation of God. Write John 1:18 below:

_____

_____

_____

_____

✏ Write John 14:7 below:

_____

_____

_____

_____

Continual Truth

Christ continues to spread His truth through the ministry of His Church. As people study the finished Word of God, He moves them to share His truth and love with the rest of the world. The Church exists not only for the encouragement and growth of believers, but also to reach unbelievers with the gospel.

Now that we have a complete and sufficient body of Scripture, we no longer need the signs of foretold events to point us in the right direction. We have everything we need to learn about God, grow in that knowledge, and trust His work in the future. Scripture condemns anyone who adds to or subtracts from this body of prophecy (Rev. 22:18–19). God reveals His authority through His finished Word, not through the false prophecies of power-hungry people today.

Christ as Priest

Through His office of High Priest, Christ acts as the mediator between a holy God and guilty, sinful people.

His Qualifications

✎ Write Hebrews 5:1–2 below:

_____

_____

_____

_____

_____

_____

These verses describe a high priest's qualifications. Other passages in Hebrews describe how Christ alone meets these requirements perfectly.

Fellowship with Humanity

✎ Write Hebrews 2:7 below:

_____

_____

_____

_____

Christ became human yet still remained God.

Authority from God

✎ Write Hebrews 5:4–5 below:

_____

_____

_____

_____

_____

_____

_____

Priests under God's Law could not appoint themselves. Their position was granted by God. Jesus therefore represented the Father, who appointed Him to be our High Priest forever, in the same priestly order as the ancient Melchizedek (6:5), who served even before the Old Testament Law was revealed.

Holiness

✎ Write Hebrews 7:25–26 below:

_____
_____
_____
_____
_____
_____
_____
_____
_____

Christ communes with the perfect Father *and* sinful humanity, yet He remains holy. He is still the perfect, exalted One, and He is eminently qualified to be our High Priest forever.

His Capabilities

✎ Summarize what the following verses teach that Christ can do for us:

- Hebrews 2:18

_____
_____

- Hebrews 4:15

_____
_____

- Hebrews 7:25

_____
_____

Christ is the ultimate solution for every one of our problems. He can help us escape every temptation, see beyond every heartache, find grace in every weakness, and show love always.

Christ as King

Revelation 19:16 explains that Christ is King of Kings and Lord of Lords. He is the sovereign ruler of all history, the One who will remain standing when all other kingdoms, empires, cultures, and civilizations have collapsed into dust. As Gabriel explained to Mary before the birth of Jesus, His kingdom will never come to an end.

Those of us still caught in the tides of history may find ourselves worrying about the rise and fall of nations and countries. We can identify with Belshazzar, King of Babylon, who received a shock while throwing a party for his friends.

During the feast, Belshazzar and his guests used a few dishes that had been sanctified for use in God's Temple—as a sort of backhanded blasphemy. As the reveling stretched on, a disembodied hand suddenly appeared and began writing on the wall of the palace. The message read "MENE, MENE, TEKEL, UPHARSIN." The words seemed close to Aramaic, but no one could understand their meaning.

The king eventually called Daniel, one of his Jewish counselors, to interpret the message.

✎ What did Daniel say the words meant (Dan. 5:25–28)?

- MENE: _____
  _____

- TEKEL: _____
  _____

- PERES: _____
  _____

This is true of all human civilizations. Like all people, cultures fail to reflect the holiness of God, and so all of them must come to ruin. God numbers their days, and He is not surprised when they fall.

✐ Read Psalm 2:1–4. According to verse 4, how does God respond to those kings and nations that rebel against Him?

_____

_____

Christ is our Prophet, Priest, and King. And in a lesser way, we too are prophets, priests, and kings.

✐ We are prophets in the sense that we share God's Word with others. In Numbers 11:29, what did Moses wish that God would someday do?

_____

_____

_____

✐ We are also priests. Because of Christ's sacrifice, we have fellowship directly with the Father. How does 1 Peter 2:5 describe us?

_____

_____

_____

_____

We can therefore pray for others and ourselves, representing others before God by pleading with Him to encourage, to bless, and to strengthen them.

✐ Finally, as members of God's family, we are also kings, in a sense. According to Revelation 5:10, how will we serve with Christ in His future kingdom?

_____

_____

We have no authority in and of ourselves, but as we submit our will to God's will, He will work through us, the representatives of His power and grace.

Notes from the Teacher's Lesson

Christ as Prophet

- His Prophethood:

  ○ Defined:

    _____

    _____

  ○ Stated: _____

- The characteristics of Christ as Prophet (Matt. 7:28-29):

    Christ taught truth with authority. He *is* absolute Truth.

- The significance of Christ as Prophet (John 17:20–26):

    He came to Earth to reveal God the Father to humanity.

Christ as Priest

- His Priesthood:

  ○ Defined:

    _____

    _____

  ○ Stated: _____

- The characteristics of Christ as Priest:

    Christ's sacrifice is complete. His was a sacrifice made once, and once only (Heb. 7:26–27). Christ listens to our prayers and represents us before God, who sees in us the righteousness of Christ (Rom. 8:31–39).

- The significance of Christ as Priest:

    As joint-heirs with Christ, we have the standing to approach God not only with thankfulness and humility, but also with the confidence that He loves us and will care for us.

Christ as King

- His Kingship:

    ○ Defined:

    _____

    _____

    ○ Stated: _____

- The characteristics of Christ as King:

    ○ His rule is internal and spiritual

    ○ One day, His rule will also be external and physical (Phil. 2:10–11)

- The significance of Christ as King:

    Because Christ is King, we know that we can live victorious lives as long as we acknowledge His supremacy.

Application Activities

1. Record a providence from your life or from broader, recent history that demonstrates to you the rule of Christ over this world.

2. Read the Book of Hebrews, and then list and summarize at least three ways in which Christ's priesthood is superior to the priesthood established by Old Testament Law.

3. Read Percy B. Shelley's poem "Ozymandias," and summarize its meaning in two or three paragraphs.

4. Identify and list six people that Scripture explicitly calls a prophet or prophetess, and briefly summarize the ministry of each. Include in your list at least one more person that Scripture does not call prophetic, but who spoke God's truth nevertheless.

CHAPTER 28

Christ's Deity

"The Scripture is clear for it. He is called the mighty God (Isa. 9:6). And in Him dwells the fullness of the Godhead (Col. 2:9). He is of the same nature and essence with the Father. . . . Is God the Father called Almighty? So is Christ (Rev. 1:8). Is God the Father the heart-searcher? So is Christ (John 2:25). Is God the Father omnipresent? So is Christ. (John 3:13). Christ as God was then in heaven, when as man He was upon the earth."

—Thomas Watson, *A Body of Divinity*

In the beginning, we read in John 1, the Word was with God, and the Word was God. Though expressed simply, these two facets of the same truth have frustrated all human attempts to define or explain them. How can Christ *be* God, yet also somehow be *distinct* from the Father and the Spirit?

Like so many biblical descriptions of God, we find in Christ's deity a riddle only His Person can solve. The importance of this truth, however, is clear—to know God, we must know Christ. He is the way, the truth, and the life; He is the light of the world; He is the door we must enter. If we have seen Christ, we have seen the Father. We may not fully understand this truth, but we can trust God and continue to explore His character until the day He gives us a perfect perspective.

So having studied the history and offices of Jesus Christ, we now focus on His Person. Who is this One who could dispel storms, yet submitted Himself to a humble life? What kind of Person could teach, inspire, heal, and feed thousands of people, yet choose to be convicted by an angry mob?

This knowledge is more precious than any other. As Paul wrote in Philippians 3:8, we can count everything else as a loss compared to the treasure of knowing Jesus. All things seem like rubbish before this incalculable wealth.

In this lesson, we'll study the basic truth of Christ's Person—His deity. He *is* the eternal, holy God.

Student Work

Denials of Christ's Deity

Upon Christ's deity rests all the rest of His teaching. If He was not God, His doctrine, ministry, and sacrifice would seem like the work of a madman. It makes sense, therefore, that enemies of Christ would continue to attack this point throughout history:

- The scribes and Pharisees became most angry when Jesus taught that He was God. It was because of this teaching that they repeatedly tried to crucify Him.

- A number of pseudo-Christian sects denied Christ's deity shortly after the first century. Among them were the *Ebionites*, some of whom thought that Jesus was simply another Jewish prophet, while others thought that He was some kind of spirit masquerading as a human.

- Arius, a preacher in the fourth century, tried to dissect the doctrine of Christ's deity, while still claiming that the Scriptures were true. This line of argument proved more attractive over time because it allowed false teachers to deny Christ without telling people to dismiss the Bible outright. Scholars often call the followers of Arius *Arians*.

- Socinus, an Italian Roman Catholic who joined the Protestant movement in the sixteenth century, found the doctrine of the Trinity so difficult that he denied it completely—denying also, like Arius, the deity of Christ. He organized anti-Trinitarian groups in Poland, and his followers were called *Socinians*.

- As theologians grappled with the interaction between science and faith through the nineteenth and twentieth centuries, many of them came to deny doctrines that did not fit within human rational frameworks. For people who preferred a distant God that did not interfere with human history, or for those who considered the Bible a flawed document written solely by people, it became convenient to deny that Christ was God.

Various groups today also disagree over the identity of Christ.

- **Some people call Him the Son of God**—that is, a literal son born from a literal father. This view represents a basic misunderstanding of "Son" as the image or representative of God. Jesus is no more the biological Son of God than He was the biological Son of a man (Matt. 8:20) or the immediate Son of David (Matt. 22:42). Rather, Christ was *of the same order as* God.

- **Some people call Him a great teacher.** They believe that we should respect and follow His teaching, but not worship Him. Yet if He blasphemed the Father by falsely claiming to be God, would He truly be worthy of our respect?

- **Some people call Him a good man.** They believe that He was a good example of kindness, sincerity, thoughtfulness, and love. Yet Christ used every act of healing and service to show others their need of *Him*. The Samaritan woman at the well needed the true, living water. The lame man whose friends lowered him through the roof needed his sins forgiven. The thousands fed in the wilderness needed the Bread of Life. We'll always have the poor, Jesus told His disciples in Matthew 26:11, but Christ is more worthy of our attention. We should reach out to help those with physical and emotional needs, but we must not forget that their greatest need is spiritual. Only Christ can meet that need.

The doctrine of Christ's deity is the test of any group that calls itself Christian. If Christ was not God but merely human, then we find ourselves following just another human—someone no more qualified to save us than we are. If Christ is merely some off-shoot of God, then He contradicts the unity of God as taught in the Old Testament.

Confirming Christ's Deity

As discussed in previous lessons, Scripture makes clear that Christ is God, co-equal with the Father and the Spirit.

Scriptural Statements That He Is God

✎ Read the following verses. Summarize the phrase that asserts Christ's deity.

- John 1:1

  _____

- John 20:28

  _____

- Romans 9:5

  _____

- Philippians 2:6

  _____

- Titus 2:13

  _____

- 1 John 5:20

  _____

Divine Names Applied to Him

As noted earlier in this study, we can see divine names given to Christ in the prophecies and Scripture that describe His work.

✎ Write the names given to Christ that state or indicate His deity.

- Isaiah 9:6—_____
- Isaiah 40:3—_____
- Jeremiah 23:5–6—_____
- Hebrews 1:8—_____

Divine Attributes Ascribed to Him

✎ The following passages show some of the divine attributes of Christ. God alone possesses this kind of power and majesty. List the attribute or attributes noted in each set of passages.

- Isaiah 9:6; John 1:1–2; Revelation 1:8—_____

- Matthew 18:20; 28:20; John 3:13—_____

- John 2:24–25; Revelation 2:23—_____

- Isaiah 9:6; Philippians 3:21; Revelation 1:8—_____

- Hebrews 13:8—_____

Divine Works Performed by Him

Jesus Christ proved His deity by doing things that only God could do. Read the following verses, and match each reference with the act that Christ performed.

John 1:3, 10	**A.** Forgives sin
John 11:43–44	**B.** Created the world
Mark 2:7–10	**C.** Raised the dead
Ephesians 1:22–23	**D.** Judges humanity
John 17:2	**E.** Gives eternal life
2 Timothy 4:1	**F.** Rules and sustains the Church

Divine Honor Paid to Him

✎ Christ accepted reverence and honor that should only have been given to God. Summarize the honor showed to Christ in each of the following passages.

- Matthew 28:19

_____

_____

_____

- John 5:23

  _____

  _____

  _____

- John 14:1

  _____

  _____

  _____

- Hebrews 1:6

  _____

  _____

  _____

· ·

Notes from the Teacher's Lesson

Christ's Deity Defined

- _____

  _____

  _____

  _____

Christ's Deity Stated

- He is _____ (John 1:1; 20:28).

- He is a member of the _____ (Matt. 28:19–20).

- He is the _____ of the Old Testament (Zech. 12:8–10, Rev. 1:7).

- He is the Angel of Jehovah (Gen. 16:7–14; 22:11–19).

  ○ The Angel of Jehovah is Jehovah-God.

  ○ The Angel of Jehovah is distinct from God (Gen. 24:7).

  ○ The Angel of Jehovah no longer appears after Christ's birth.

The Significance of Christ's Deity

- The inspiration of _____

- The truth of Christ's teaching (John 8:46–59)

- Our _____ (Heb. 7:23–28)

- The _____ of our worship (Matt. 4:10; Phil. 2:9–11)

Application Activities

1. Read Hebrews 1. List all of the things you see in that passage concerning the deity and person of Jesus Christ.

2. Record a providence from your life that inspired gratitude for your salvation in Christ.

3. In one page, summarize and evaluate the core beliefs of one of the following religious groups, paying particular attention to their views concerning the deity of Christ. Note that people in each group today may not entirely agree with the original teaching of the group's founder, and many doctrines vary widely from person to person.

   - Arianism
   - Socinianism
   - Christian Science
   - Jehovah's Witnesses
   - Mormonism

CHAPTER 29

Christ's Humanity

"He became what we are that He might make us what He is."

—Athanasius, *The New Book of Christian Quotations*

Jesus Christ is both fully God and fully human. As God in the flesh, He endured the same kind of hardship and suffering that we face, except He always shone with perfect love and truth. In Christ we see the perfect example of righteousness—proof positive that we humans, by His grace, can reflect God despite our weakness and imperfection.

The previous lesson noted that some groups, struggling to understand how God could become flesh, deny the deity of Christ. Other groups simply deny His humanity, saying that He was a spirit who appeared as a human. Yet as we've seen, Scripture affirms *both* His humanity and His deity, as impossible as that might seem. It takes faith to believe both doctrines, and wisdom to express them well.

Some Christians, however, emphasize Christ's humanity to the exclusion of His deity, presenting Him as a common friend or buddy. They might elaborate on stories of His earthly ministry, introducing whimsy or anachronism to entertain children. Some writers—dating back even to the second century— wrote entire books of make-believe stories about Jesus' childhood. Yet children notice the details of stories far more than many adults realize, so we should not confuse fact with fiction.

It is important to present stories of Christ with the same care and accuracy shown in the original Gospels. Jesus is not some folk hero or Greek demigod whose exploits can be modified and retold to suit our own message. He is a true, living, historical figure, who chose every word and action carefully. He is God, and we should no more toy with the record of His ministry than we should edit the doctrine of Romans. The Gospel writers may have at times summarized Christ's messages to fit the theme of each book, but they did so under the inspiration of the Spirit, and they did not add to what Jesus taught.

When studying the humanity of Christ, we should not forget His deity or the reverence He deserves. Christ became human to demonstrate the grace and truth of God. We should therefore approach this doctrine with the respect due His entire Person.

Student Work

Marks of Christ's Humanity

Jesus is God from eternity past, but He was not always human. He became flesh at a particular point in time. Now, after His incarnation, He is the God-Man whom we trust for salvation.

Scripture makes clear Christ's identity as human. Note four of the clearest marks of Christ's humanity:

His Human Ancestry

We find two genealogies of Christ in the New Testament, one in Matthew 1:1–17 and the other in Luke 3:23–38. Matthew traced the *paternal* line from Abraham to Jesus' earthly father, Joseph. Though Jesus had no biological father, Matthew emphasizes His place in the royal line of David to demonstrate Christ's fulfillment of Old Testament prophecy.

Luke, however, traced Christ's *maternal* genealogy through Mary back to Adam. This line emphasizes Christ's humanity, though He was born without a sinful nature.

Note the kind of people that God blessed to be ancestors of Jesus:

- **Jacob**—a trickster
- **Judah**—a man who allowed his own brother to be sold into slavery
- **Rahab**—a prostitute from Jericho who rescued Israelite spies
- **Ruth**—another Gentile from Moab

- **Bathsheba**—the mistress of King David who later taught her son, Solomon
- **Rehoboam, Abijah, Joram**—all wicked kings

Christ represented all of humanity, yet He still met the royal qualifications of the Messiah. He descended from sinners, yet He was perfect. He took on our form to die in our place.

His Human Appearance

Scripture gives us no clear description of Christ's appearance during His earthly ministry, but we can surmise perhaps that He looked like the other Jewish males in His day, with a beard, dark hair, and light-brown skin. It's impossible, however, to provide an accurate description or image of His features—nor is it necessary.

✎ In each of the following passages, how did people see Christ? What did He simply appear to be?

- Luke 24:13–18—_____
- John 4:9—_____
- John 20:15—_____

Except for the time He revealed His glory at the Transfiguration (Matt. 17:1–9), Christ looked like a normal human male. He did not walk around with a halo over His head, nor did He have an aura or glow surrounding Him.

His Human Infirmities

Like every other man, Christ endured the same human problems and limitations, with one major exception—He had no sin.

✎ For each of the following passages, write what Christ faced as a human.

- Matthew 4:2—_____
- Matthew 26:36–40—_____
- John 4:6—_____
- John 11:35—_____

- John 19:28—_____

- Hebrews 2:9–10; 12:2—_____

Christ submitted Himself to these human limitations for the same reason He submitted Himself to His heavenly Father and to His earthly parents—to be an example for us. The all-powerful God of the universe still clung to the Father, using this divine communion and unity to model the communion and unity that we believers can have with God.

✎ Write John 17:20–21 below:

_____

_____

_____

_____

_____

_____

_____

_____

As Christ struggled with the knowledge of His upcoming death, He poured out His heart to the Father. His desire in that moment was for us to know the love and joy that come only from a relationship with God.

His Human Names

✎ In John 1:51, Christ called Himself the Son of _____. We find this phrase at least 29 times in Matthew, 14 times in Mark, 26 times in Luke, and 13 times in John.

And Christ did not shed His humanity when He ascended into heaven. He is still very much human today.

✎ At the moment of his martyrdom in Acts 7:54–60, who saw Christ standing as a human at the right hand of God? _____

John also refers to Christ's humanity in his descriptions of Jesus in the Book of Revelation (1:13).

Notes from the Teacher's Lesson

Christ's Humanity Defined

- _____
  _____
  _____
  _____

- We affirm Jesus Christ's . . .

  ○ _____—He is absolutely God.

  ○ _____—He is absolutely human.

  ○ _____—He is one Person.

  ○ _____—He has two natures, each
  distinct yet inseparable.

- Major errors concerning Christ's Person:

  ○ Docetism

  _____
  _____
  _____
  _____

  ○ Arianism

  _____
  _____
  _____
  _____

  ○ Nestorianism

  _____
  _____
  _____
  _____

- ○ Eutychianism

  _____

  _____

  _____

  _____

  _____

  _____

  _____

  _____

- Most errors in the early church arose from one of two issues:
  - ○ A denial of Scripture
  - ○ An insistence on explaining the exact mechanics of God's work

Christ's Humanity Stated

_____

The Significance of Christ's Humanity

- It qualifies Him as our _____ (1 Tim. 2:5–6).

- It provides _____ over death (Heb. 2:14–18; 1 Cor. 15:55–57).

- It provides us a _____ High Priest (Heb. 2:16–18; Isa. 53:2–7).

Application Activities

1. Read Isaiah 53, and record your impressions of what Christ must have faced as a human on Earth.

2. Record a personal providence in which Christ provided you the grace to endure a hardship. Give an example from the Gospels that shows Christ facing a similar trial.

3. Read Luke 2:51–52, and summarize what you believe these verses teach about the humanity of Christ. In what way did Christ serve as an example for you, personally?

4. Find a Bible storybook for children, and choose a story intended to reflect a narrative within Scripture. In one page, describe how closely the story sticks with the original narrative.

   - What details have been changed or added?

   - How do these changes affect the overall theme of the story?

   - Why do you think the author of the story made these changes?

   - Which additions do you believe are acceptable, and which are unhelpful?

5. Choose a narrative within Scripture, and write a story following that narrative, with an audience of five- or six-year-olds in mind. In a paragraph following your story, briefly summarize how you presented the original narrative to preserve accuracy while also meeting the needs of your listeners.

CHAPTER 30
Christ's Names

"Other names are dear, but His is dearer."

—Herbert Lockyer, *All the Men of the Bible*

"What's in a name?" asked Juliet in Shakespeare's famous play. "That which we call a rose / By any other name would smell as sweet." Juliet assured her lover, Romeo, that his family's reputation meant nothing to her. Yet the flames of their families' conflict would eventually engulf them both.

There's a lot in name—it's a symbol of our identity, our community, our character. Some names reflect our heritage, while some are unique. Some names reflect principles or ideals. Some names are given, some are earned, but all reflect who we are to our family, friends, and the world at large. Our names represent our public personality—they're shorthand for all the characteristics and actions that affect how people view us.

A parent might say to a child before going out in public, "Remember who you are!" We can easily damage the reputation tied to our family name, just as we can misrepresent Christ by claiming to be a Christian while failing to reflect His truth and love.

A popular trend of the late 1990s was to show stickers, bracelets, and other paraphernalia with the letters *WWJD*—shorthand for "What would Jesus do?" These served not only as reminders to reflect Christ, but also as a way to publicly identify with the Christian faith. Other Christian symbols have served similar roles—like the cross or the fish-shaped *ichthys*.

But by bearing these symbols, we also bear the responsibility to *act* like Christ. What would you think of a rude, aggressive driver with a Christian bumper sticker? How would you view a family who places a cross in front of their house, yet treats their neighbors coldly? Religious hypocrites are the worst hypocrites, because the standard they claim is so much higher.

The truth is, regardless of whether we sport a t-shirt, a sticker, or a sign, we believers all represent Christ, and we must reflect Him to the world. We should proudly identify with Him, but we should also humbly acknowledge our failures and faithfully share truth and love with others.

Jesus Christ, our highest example, has always lived up to His names. Scholars have cataloged at least 150 names for Him in Scripture, and He meets the righteous expectations of those titles perfectly. We'll study just a few in this lesson, but you could spend a lifetime meditating on the grace that shines through this topic.

Student Work

Other Names of Christ

The teacher's lesson for this chapter covers the names *Jesus*, *Christ*, and *the Lord of Glory*. We'll quickly look over a few more.

Old Testament Names

✎ Write the name, title, or role of Christ that you find in each passage.

- Numbers 24:17—_____

- Deuteronomy 18:15—_____

- Job 19:25—_____

- Isaiah 7:14—_____

- Isaiah 9:6—_____
  _____

- Zechariah 6:12—_____

New Testament Names

Christic as the Great I AM (John 8:58)

✎ Read Exodus 3:14 again. What name did God use for Himself? _____

As noted in previous lessons, this name indicates *eternal present tense*. Unlike us, God is not bound to the linear sequence of time. He has direct access to the past, the present, and the future, and He transcends all human limitations and conceptions.

Therefore, as the eternal God, Christ never began, will never end, and is completely self-sufficient. He was right to claim the name of *Yahweh* because it was He who spoke to Moses through the burning bush.

✎ Read the following passages: Ephesians 3:19; Hebrews 13:8; and 1 John 3:1. Which passage best expresses the eternality of Christ?

_____

✎ How could these two things be eternal, if Christ was not?

- In Christ, God revealed His eternal _____ (Eph. 3:11).

- Christ is also worthy of _____ forever (Heb. 13:21).

✎ As God, Christ was completely self-sufficient:

- When a wedding ran out of _____, He provided a fresh batch from barrels of water (John 2:1–11).

- When thousands of people needed to eat, He provided them food from just _____ (Matt. 14:13–21).

- When He had no boat to reach His disciples on the Sea of Galilee, He simply _____ (Matt. 14:22–33).

- When the disciples needed a _____ to pay taxes, He provided one from a fish (Matt. 17:24–27).

He was dependent on nothing and no one else to accomplish His work. As God in the flesh, He bore the full power and approval of the Father.

Christic as the Source of All Good

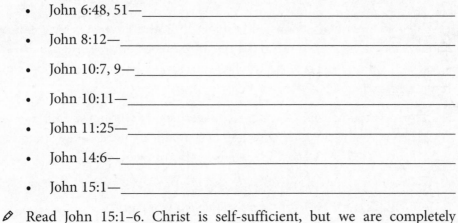

✎ What did Christ claim to be in each of the following verses—that is, what do we have through Him?

- John 6:48, 51—_____

- John 8:12—_____

- John 10:7, 9—_____

- John 10:11—_____

- John 11:25—_____

- John 14:6—_____

- John 15:1—_____

✎ Read John 15:1–6. Christ is self-sufficient, but we are completely dependent on Him for life and grace. According to verse 4, what must we do to avoid drying up and dying?

_____

Only through Christ can we live and bear fruit. We must seek to know Him, and once we've found Him, we must stay connected to His Word and His fellowship, changing our thoughts to mirror His thoughts, celebrating His love with other believers, and living a life that reflects His love and truth.

Why do we keep thinking that we need the world, with all its pride, conflict, ambition, petty amusements, abuse, and shame? As the Source of everything good, Christ is all that we truly need.

Notes from the Teacher's Lesson

Jesus

- Defined:

  _____

  _____

  _____

- Stated: _____

- Significance of the name *Jesus*:

  ○ This salvation is for us (Matt. 1:21).

  ○ This salvation is from God (Jonah 2:9; Ps. 3:8; Ps. 37:39).

    ○ Isaiah 43:11 – Beside Jehovah is no other savior.

    ○ Isaiah 45:21–22 – No other god or savior exists.

  ○ This salvation inspires praise.

Christ

- Defined:

  _____

  _____

  _____

- Stated: _____

- The Old Testament described the Messiah as the following:

  ○ The offspring of Abraham and of David (Gen. 22:18; 2 Sam. 7:16)

  ○ A baby born to a young woman, a virgin (Isa. 7:14)

  ○ A baby born in Bethlehem (Mic. 5:2)

  ○ A great king (Jer. 23:5–6; Isa. 9:7)

  ○ A priest forever (Ps. 110:4)

  ○ A prophet like Moses (Deut. 18:15)

- One who would preach good tidings to the meek and the poor, as well as liberty to captives (Isa. 61:1–2)

- One who would comfort the mourning and heal the brokenhearted (Isa. 61:1–2)

- One who would publish His gospel first in the land of Zebulon and Naphtali, in Galilee of the Gentiles, and then throughout the coasts of Israel (Isa. 9:1–2)

- One who would arrive at Jerusalem humbly, riding on a colt (Zech. 9:9)

- One who would have a forerunner with the power of Elijah (Mal. 4:5–6)

- One who would make the blind see, the deaf hear, the mute speak, and the lame leap for joy (Isa. 29:18; Isa. 35:5–6)

- One rejected by many, including much of His own people (Ps. 118:22; Isa. 8:14; 53:3)

- One hated without cause, accused by false witnesses, betrayed by a close friend for thirty pieces of silver (Ps. 35:11; 41:9; Zech. 11:13)

- One used in a barbarous and shameful manner, buffeted, spat upon (Isa. 50:6)

- One despised, afflicted, one who endured sorrows, accustomed to grief (Isa. 53:3)

- One who would be pierced, crushed, and punished (Isa. 53:5)

- One led like a lamb to the slaughter, not opening His mouth (Isa. 53:7)

- One whose bones would somehow not be broken (Ps. 34:20)

- One who would cry "My God, My God, why have you forsaken me?" (Ps. 22:1), whose clothing would be taken and gambled away while His bones stretched out from His flesh (vv. 17–18)

- One numbered with transgressors (Isa. 53:12), and laid in the grave of a rich man (v. 9)

- One who would rise again before His body had seen corruption (Ps. 16:10)
- One who would ascend to heaven to sit at the right hand of the Father (Ps. 68:18; 110:1)

- Significance of the name *Christ*:

  To identify Jesus as Christ is to assign Him all the power and glory of the Messiah described in the Old Testament.

Lord of Glory

- Defined:
  - *Lord* – _____
  - *Glory* – _____
  - *Lord of Glory* – _____
    _____

- Stated: _____
  - His _____ glory (John 1:14)
  - His glory as the _____ (Phil. 2:9–11)

- Significance of the name *Lord of Glory*:
  - It is a guarantee of glory for us (John 17:22).
  - We can behold His glory now (2 Cor. 3:12–18).
  - He outshines all else.

Application Activities

1. Read John 17, and record all of the things that Jesus Christ has done and will continue to do for those who trust Him. What do you learn about Christ in this passage?

2. Record a providence of any kind in which God provided for a person's needs. Describe the need and the way God met it.

3. List at least a dozen names for Christ, and briefly summarize the meaning and/or context of each. Include a Scripture reference for each name. Cite any sources you use, as well.

4. Write a paragraph summarizing the origins of the term *Christian*. Then list at least three other terms that have been used to describe those who trust Christ. Briefly summarize the origin and meaning of each term, citing any sources you use.

UNIT 6
The Holy Spirit

"The Third Person in the Trinity is the Holy Ghost, who proceeds from the Father and the Son, whose work is to illuminate the mind, and enkindle sacred emotions."

—Thomas Watson, *A Body of Divinity*

CHAPTER 31

Who the Holy Spirit Is

"The Holy Spirit is a living Person and should be treated as a person. We must never think of Him as a blind energy nor as an impersonal force."

—A. W. Tozer, "The Divine Conquest," *A Treasury of A. W. Tozer*

As noted in the teacher's lesson for this chapter, the Holy Spirit is often the most misunderstood member of the Trinity. So much false teaching has surrounded this doctrine that even thoughtful Christians spend more time pointing out what He is *not* than who He actually *is*.

But the Spirit plays a vital role in the life of each believer. Contrary to the descriptions of some people, He is not some vague energy or force—He is a real, literal member of the Trinity, with a will and a personality.

Why might some be tempted to think of the Spirit as an impersonal force? Because a force can be used or manipulated to suit our own ends. Who wouldn't want the same kind of power shown in the apostles after Christ's ascension? They could speak other languages, heal the sick, cast out demons, and perform other miracles.

We can understand, therefore, why Simon the sorcerer offered Peter and John money in exchange for the power to use the Holy Spirit (Acts 8:9–25). Simon was understandably amazed at these marvels—but he did not appreciate their source in a Person.

So Peter told Simon, bluntly, that the sorcerer's money could *die with him*. Simon had profaned God's gifts by assuming they could be bought, sold, and bartered. Like Ananias and Sapphira in Acts 5, he thought that he could buy himself a position as some sort of super-Christian. It's difficult to overstate the sheer blasphemy of treating God like just another tool of rich and powerful people.

Fortunately, Simon accepted Peter's rebuke and understood his error. Like him, we must realize that the Spirit works *through us*—we do not direct Him like some magic power.

Some people will always use God's name without His permission—claiming His authority for themselves and putting His approval on doctrines He never taught us. Beware of anyone who dogmatically puts God's authority behind something not clearly taught in Scripture, and beware of those who define God's blessing in terms of money and wealth.

If we wanted a god who just gave us *more stuff*, then we could worship a billionaire or a tyrant. But we need more than that. We need grace, joy, patience, hope—things only the Spirit can provide.

As we abide in God's Word, He will give us the love and truth we need to outshine this world's darkness. As we follow the leading of the Spirit, accepting and celebrating His work through people of all backgrounds, He will build a Church that does not reflect the political, social, racial, and economic hierarchies we see in the world. Instead, as Christ prayed for us in John 17, we will be one together in God.

Student Work

Further Statements of the Spirit's Deity

Expanding on what was taught in the teacher's lesson, we'll consider the ways that Scripture presents the Holy Spirit as God. The following are some of the clearest examples:

His Person

Scripture Refers to Him with Personal Pronouns

Read John 16:7–15. How many times does the writer reference the Holy Spirit with a personal pronoun, such as *He* or *Himself*? _____

He Has the Characteristics of a Person

Match each of the following verses with the appropriate action or characteristic.

John 14:26	**A.** He speaks.
Romans 8:14	**B.** He has knowledge and intelligence.
Romans 15:30	**C.** He can be grieved or disrespected.
1 Corinthians 2:10–12; Romans 8:27	**D.** He loves.
1 Corinthians 12:11	**E.** He teaches.
Ephesians 4:30	**F.** He has a will.
Revelation 2:7	**G.** He leads, or guides.

He Worked Personally Through the Early Church

The Holy Spirit not only calls people to serve God, He enables them to do so. The earliest missionaries relied heavily on His wisdom and guidance.

✐ Summarize what the Holy Spirit did in each of the following passages:

- Acts 13:2—_____

  _____

- Acts 16:6–7—_____

  _____

- Acts 20:28—_____

  _____

We must be sensitive to the leading of the Spirit. He will guide us as we . . .

- Abide in God's Word, understanding His love and truth

- Obey God's commandments as they apply to this stage of our lives

- Develop and mature—physically, mentally, emotionally, and spiritually

- Desire God's will, aligning ourselves with His desires and asking Him to guide our thoughts

- Accept His love and truth, as shown through His Word and the advice of godly people

Our ministry is not actually our own—it's His. He works through us, and we should acknowledge His sole authority at every step. We are stewards of His gifts.

His Equality with God

Scripture Calls Him God

The teacher's lesson noted two Old Testament passages that referred to *the Lord*—but, when repeated in the New Testament, exchanged *the Lord* for *Holy Spirit*. It's clear, then, that the New Testament writers considered the Holy Spirit to be God.

✎ How does Peter call the Holy Spirit God in Acts 5:3–4?

_____

_____

_____

Scripture Associates Him with the Father and the Son

As noted in previous lessons, God the Father, Son, and Holy Spirit are all mentioned together in a number of different verses.

✎ Before Christ ascended, He instructed His disciples to go and make yet more disciples. How were they to baptize these followers into the Church (Matt. 28:19)?

_____

Christ expected His followers to acknowledge and respect the Trinity.

Scripture Ascribes to Him the Attributes of the Father and the Son

Match each passage with the attribute it indicates.

Genesis 1:2; Luke 1:35	**A.** Omnipotence
Psalm 139:7–10	**B.** Omniscience
Romans 15:30	**C.** Omnipresence
1 Corinthians 2:10–11	**D.** Eternality
Hebrews 9:14	**E.** Truth
1 John 5:6	**F.** Love

Notes from the Teacher's Lesson

The Doctrine of the Holy Spirit Defined

- _____
  _____
  _____
  _____
  _____

- What the Holy Spirit is not:
  _____
  _____
  _____
  _____
  _____
  _____

- What the Holy Spirit is:
  - A member of the _____

  - A Person _____ with God the Father
    and the Son

  - A Person _____ from the Father and the Son

The Doctrine of the Holy Spirit Stated

- The Holy Spirit is a Person.

  _____

- The Holy Spirit is God.
  - The Lord _____ (Isa. 6:8–10; Acts 28:25–27)

  - The LORD _____ (Exo. 16:7–8; Heb. 3:7–9)

- The Holy Spirit is distinct from the Father and the Son.

  _____

The Significance of the Holy Spirit

- His Person
  - He can be _____ (Eph. 4:30).
  - He can be _____ (Heb. 10:29).
- His Deity (Heb. 3:7–19)

· ·

Application Activities

1. Record a providence—either biblical or personal—in which the Holy Spirit clearly led someone through a decision or ministry.

2. Record at least a dozen examples of the Holy Spirit featured as a Person in Scripture. Briefly summarize what each passage teaches us about Him.

3. Read Chapters 1–5 of Book III ("What the Bible Teaches About the Holy Spirit") from *What the Bible Teaches* by R. A. Torrey. Write a brief outline of the topics, ideas, and passages covered by these chapters.

4. Select a major decision that you know you will face in the next seven years, and outline how you intend to seek God's wisdom and guidance to make your choice.

   - What resources are at your disposal?
   - What purposes, goals, and principles should you keep in mind?
   - What can you do to prepare now?

CHAPTER 32

The Creative Work of the Spirit

"Other things maintain life, He gives life. Who would put anything in balance with the Deity? Who would weigh a feather against a mountain of gold?"

—Thomas Watson, *A Body of Divinity*

Traditional philosophies often defined beauty as an expression of two qualities—*order* and *meaning*. From this perspective, an object or picture is beautiful to the extent that it artfully expresses the message of its maker. A person is therefore beautiful because he or she reflects the image and work of the Creator.

Modern philosophers, however, often define beauty simply as *attractiveness*. With this view, we call things beautiful because we want to possess or consume them, or otherwise be near them. We can find this kind of beauty not only in high art, music, or nature, but also in a random splatter of paint on a wall.

This modern sense of beauty, explored by Western artists and writers in the mid-twentieth century, emphasizes the meaning interpreted by a work's *audience*, not its creator. A viewer or reader can decide what the work means, and the author's intent is just one more opinion among many. This idea arose to acknowledge the fact that we all view beauty differently. However, this thinking also proved attractive to people who denied the existence of any higher meaning at all. When we no longer view the universe as a work of art by God, we tend to lower our expectations for art created by humans.

Yet God is a master artist, a master storyteller, and a brilliant architect. No one compelled Him to fill the universe with such terror and beauty. No one asked Jesus to teach in the form of stories and parables. No one could possibly imagine the complex expression of holiness, power, and goodness that is the gospel. God filled His Word with poetry, psalms, prophecies, genealogies, letters of encouragement, arguments, debates, barely articulated descriptions of heaven, and even an entire book of songs celebrating the intimacy shared by a husband and a wife. God expressed His love and truth in all of this, and we cannot help but acknowledge the beauty of His work.

The common response to beauty is the desire to create *more*. As we see beauty in nature and art, we want to capture some of that same good in our own work. As we see the goodness of God shining through people, we want to serve them. As the Spirit illumines His truth in the Word, we want to share that truth with others.

This activity can involve study and hard work, but it's more than worth it to become a vessel used by the Master Potter to magnify His majesty.

Student Work

The teacher's lesson for this chapter examines the Spirit's work primarily within Creation. Here we'll briefly cover His work in the Old Testament, as well as His revelation of truth throughout the Scriptures.

The Spirit in the Old Testament

Selective Indwelling

Peter's sermon at Pentecost marked the permanent indwelling of the Holy Spirit in believers. Before Pentecost, however, the Holy Spirit did not reside in all of God's people. He chose a select few to demonstrate His power.

For each passage, write the name of the person said to be indwelled by the Spirit. Note that some of these statements were made by people who did not know God.

- Genesis 41:25–38—_____
- Numbers 27:18—_____
- Daniel 4:8—_____
- Judges 6:34—_____
- 1 Samuel 16:13—_____

Enablement for Service

✎ In the Old Testament, the Holy Spirit sometimes gave people special abilities to do impressive things. For each passage below, write the name of the person God enabled.

- Exodus 31:1–3—Bezaleel: What work did the Spirit enable this person to do?

  _____

  _____

  _____

- Judges 14:5–6—Samson: What did the Spirit allow this person to do?

  _____

  _____

In the New Testament and today, the Holy Spirit serves to communicate the work and character of God. Match each passage below with the name it gives the Spirit.

	John 14:17	**A.** Spirit of grace
	Romans 1:4	**B.** Spirit of holiness
	Romans 8:2	**C.** Spirit of truth
	Romans 8:15	**D.** Spirit of life
	Ephesians 1:17	**E.** Spirit of adoption
	Hebrews 10:29	**F.** Spirit of wisdom

Revelation and Inspiration

Definitions

Two terms can enhance our appreciation for God's Word:

- *Revelation*—the disclosure of previously unknown truth. The term can also refer specifically to the truth revealed.

- *Inspiration*—God's work through human authors so that, as they wrote with their own perspective and personality, they recorded God's revelation without error.

Revelation is therefore the truth that God gave us, and *inspiration* refers to the manner in which He gave this truth to us.

Authorship

The Spirit, as God, is the Author behind the revelation and inspiration of Scripture. He is the reason for the *what* and the *how* of the Bible.

✐ Match each passage below with the truth it teaches.

	2 Samuel 23:1–2	**A.** People spoke as they were moved by the Holy Spirit.
	Acts 28:25	**B.** The Spirit of the Lord spoke through David.
	2 Timothy 3:16	**C.** The Holy Spirit spoke through Isaiah.
	2 Peter 1:21	**D.** All Scripture is inspired, or "God-breathed."

Means

✐ God used various means to reveal His truth to people throughout the Bible. Read each passage below, and write the method by which God communicated His revelation.

- Genesis 20:6—_____

- Exodus 19:9—_____

- Isaiah 1:1—_____

- John 1:14—_____

Since we now have the sufficient Word of God today, we need not rely on visions or voices to know God's truth. The Scriptures are themselves a miracle, a sign that God loved us enough to preserve His message and truth through the centuries, through the countless manuscripts transcribed and compiled by imperfect people. His Word has nonetheless remained true and sure, and we can read gratefully of His grace.

Notes from the Teacher's Lesson

The Gift of Life

The Spirit of God gives life to Creation. He is the source of what animates us—what sparked humanity from inert matter into living flesh.

- The gift stated:

    - In _____ (Job 33:4)

    - In _____ (Job 34:14–15)

- The significance of this gift:

    - In our _____ (2 Cor. 5:17)

    - In our ministry to _____
      (John 15:26–27; Acts 1:8)

    - In our _____
      (Gal. 5:22–23; Eph. 5:9; Phil. 1:11)

The Gift of Beauty

The Holy Spirit did not create a teeming, chaotic mass of life. He created a world with order and meaning—that is, a world with beauty.

- The gift stated:

    - **Genesis 1:2, 2:7**—The Spirit of God formed the structure and order of the universe out of nothing, and He formed humanity out of dust.

    - **Job 26:13**—The Spirit (or breath) of God made the heavens beautiful. Note also Psalm 33:6.

    - **Job 32:6–10**—We do not gain true wisdom from age or experience—but from the Spirit of God. Only He can help us understand purpose and meaning.

- **Exodus 31:1–5; 35:30–35**—The Spirit empowered people specifically to create beautiful designs for the Tabernacle and Temple.

- **Isaiah 40:12–17**—The Spirit controls His Creation and gives it order.

- **2 Timothy 3:16; Acts 1:16; Hebrews 10:15–18**—The Holy Spirit inspired the words of Scripture, a work of beauty.

- The significance of this gift:

_____

_____

_____

_____

_____

_____

_____

_____

Application Activities

1. List and summarize at least three passages from the Bible that describe or reference the work of God's Spirit in Creation.

2. Read Chapter 6 ("The Work of the Holy Spirit") and Chapter 7 ("The Baptism with the Holy Spirit") of Book III of *What the Bible Teaches* by R. A. Torrey. Briefly outline the topics, ideas, and passages you find.

3. Write a two-page paper describing how the early church recognized the 66 books that make up the biblical canon. Rely on reputable sources, and cite any you use.

   • In what ways do you believe that God worked through this process?

   • What disagreements have you found between some of your sources?

   Note: your teacher might help you identify reputable sources.

4. Choose a book on prayer, and write a one page paper summarizing the book's perspective on the role of the Holy Spirit.

CHAPTER 33

The Holy Spirit's Work in Salvation

"Though Christ merits grace for us, it is the Holy Ghost that works it in us. Though Christ makes the purchase, it is the Holy Ghost that makes the assurance, and seals us to the day of redemption."

—Thomas Watson, *A Body of Divinity*

Ms. Jameson noted that for the last fifteen minutes of the test, Rick had seemed intently focused on his water bottle. She was glad he wanted to stay hydrated, but she wasn't sure if that was his only motivation.

Slipping quietly from her desk at the front of the classroom, she walked nonchalantly past her students toward the back. Pretending to adjust some books on a shelf, she looked again at Rick, who sat a few rows up, near the middle of the class. The other students seemed focused on their test, but Rick, as if he could detect his teacher's attention, acted almost *too* casual. He checked off another answer on his paper, then slowly reached up to his water bottle, covering part of its label with his hand.

Ms. Jameson walked up the aisle and stood by his desk. "Rick, do you want me to get a refill for you from the water cooler?"

Rick looked up and smiled awkwardly. "No thanks—I'm good."

The teacher thought to herself, *Why did I think that would work?*

To Rick, however, she said, "May I see this?"

He froze, but didn't object when she took the bottle and glanced at the label. Sure enough, it wasn't the glossy, printed plastic from the bottling company.

It was home printer paper covered in plastic tape. The label looked like a copy of what you'd find in a store—except that there were test keywords, dates, and definitions printed in tiny blue font on the back.

The teacher lowered her voice. "Rick, please see me afterward."

She took the bottle and his unfinished test back with her to her desk.

Twenty minutes later, after Rick pretended to casually lounge at his desk while the other students left the room, he walked up to his teacher's desk, eager to explain.

He tried the pity routine first, saying that he had been too busy the night before stocking shelves at his dad's store. He didn't have time to study. Ms. Jameson told him that he could have prepared long before yesterday. Besides, didn't it take some time to copy, design, and print this fake label?

Rick then did the accusation bit. The test was too difficult. The reading assignments were too long. The teacher never stopped during her lectures to explain things well.

"I've never seen you during my office hours," Ms. Jameson replied. "Nor at any of the study groups I've organized. But even if you had trouble with the material, that wouldn't justify cheating."

Rick didn't respond, but he seemed to brace for a lecture.

"I'm afraid I'm going to have to report you to Dr. Feingold. She'll speak with your parents and put this on your record. I'm not sure how this will affect your place in football."

Rick glowered at her in silence, and she stood up to leave, waiting just an extra moment to see if he'd at least apologize.

Sure enough, he muttered, "I'm sorry." Then he shuffled past her out of the room. If he was anything like the other students she caught cheating, he was probably on his way to start damage control with his parents.

Ms. Jameson didn't know if he was sorry that he cheated—or sorry that he was caught. His apology seemed liked a formality, and he showed little intention of changing his ways. Regardless, the teacher hoped that he would reach out for help soon.

She looked again at the fake label. It was an impressive job. The logo and design elements weren't pixelated, and even the test notes meshed well with the layout. Rick certainly had time and talent, but apparently no desire to study.

Ms. Jameson wasn't looking forward to her meeting with Dr. Feingold.

As we read in 2 Corinthians 7, the Holy Spirit produces the only genuine repentance. Grief, sorrow, and apologies themselves do not necessarily mark a turn toward righteousness. Repentance is an inner change—not an outward display to get us out of trouble.

In this lesson, we examine the Holy Spirit's work in salvation. The teacher's lesson covers the essential material, so the following exercises will explore the nature of the Spirit's saving work throughout the Book of Acts.

Student Work

The Outreach of the Spirit

✎ Read John 15:18–16:4. Here Christ tells His disciples what the world will be like after He has departed. Describe the opposition the disciples would face.

_____

_____

_____

_____

_____

_____

✎ Yet what would the Spirit do through the followers of Christ (15:26)?

_____

_____

The Holy Spirit would spread the gospel through the witness of Christ's disciples (Acts 1:8). We certainly couldn't do that on our own.

✎ What then happened at the feast of Pentecost? How did the Holy Spirit mark His arrival (Acts 2:1–3)?

_____

_____

_____

_____

_____

✎ What miracle did He reveal through these believers (vv. 4–11)?

_____

_____

_____

_____

With people gathered in Jerusalem from all over the world, the Holy Spirit intended to spread the good news of Christ rapidly, across boundaries the believers couldn't have crossed on their own.

✎ Peter stood up in front of the crowd and explained this mighty work as a fulfillment of a prophecy by the prophet Joel (vv. 17–21):

- God would pour out His Spirit on all _____ (v. 17).

- Both _____ and _____ would prophesy (v. 17).

- Both _____ and _____ would receive dreams or visions (v. 17)

- The Spirit would be poured out on God's _____, both male and female (v. 18).

✎ And according to verse 21, who would be saved?

_____

_____

Anyone—young or old, male or female, rich or poor—could now accept Christ and receive the Holy Spirit. God would offer His salvation to all nations, across all languages, and through every barrier that humanity used to divide itself. Anyone could now trust Christ and receive equal standing as a child of God, a joint-heir with Christ, and a vessel of the Spirit.

After Pentecost, the Spirit continued to show His power. He gave Peter courage to speak before the council (Acts 4:31), and the Spirit's wisdom in Stephen destroyed the objections of Christ's enemies (Acts 6:10). The religious leaders couldn't silence truth with their lies, so they resorted to violence, stoning Stephen and arresting others in the growing church.

Yet the Holy Spirit continued to minister through the apostles, marking their ministry with His visible presence. Today, the Spirit doesn't appear with tongues of fire or special signs—that seems to have been a way to mark God's authority behind the apostles—but He still miraculously changes hearts, turning people toward Christ.

✎ Despite all this, Peter and the other disciples still had a few prejudices holding their ministry back. Read Acts 10:9–29. What did God teach Peter through this vision?

_____

_____

_____

✎ How did Peter then begin his presentation of the gospel to a group of Gentiles? Answer by writing Acts 10:34–35 below.

_____

_____

_____

_____

_____

_____

✎ Read verses 44–48. What were Peter's companions amazed to see?

_____

_____

_____

The Holy Spirit continued to break down barriers through the rest of Acts. He could not be controlled or restricted by some select group. While some people were angry that Peter and Paul reached out to the Gentiles, others rejoiced to see God fulfill His promise to shine light to the rest of the world.

It's as if believers spend the rest of Acts scrambling *after* the Spirit—barely keeping up with His explosive work. We read about His ministry reaching out from the Middle East toward the rest of the world, through men and women, Jews and Gentiles, scholars and fishers, rich and poor, free people and slaves—sinners of every conceivable background and status.

✎ Write Galatians 3:28 below.

_____

_____

_____

_____

The apostles therefore needed great wisdom to help believers build unity despite their differences. Thankfully, the Spirit inspired much of the New Testament Scriptures specifically to show believers the common ground they can find in the gospel of grace. The Church that God built is the Church He will protect and preserve (Matt. 16:15–19).

· ·

Notes from the Teacher's Lesson

Conviction

- Defined:

_____

_____

_____

_____

- Stated: John 16:8–11

    ○ Conviction of _____ (v. 9)

    ○ Conviction of _____ (v. 10)

    ○ Conviction of _____ (v. 11)

- Significance:

    ○ We must behold God.

    ○ We must turn from sin to God.

Regeneration

- Defined:

  _____

  _____

  _____

- Stated: Titus 3:4–7
- Significance:
  - We cannot save ourselves.
  - The Spirit transforms our souls.

Indwelling

- Defined:

  _____

  _____

  _____

  _____

- Stated: John 14:16–17; 1 Corinthians 6:19
- Significance:
  - It guards against _____ (Gal. 5:16–25).
  - We are His _____ (1 Cor. 6:19).

Baptism

- Defined:

  _____

  _____

  _____

  Note: This should not be confused with the ritual of water baptism, nor is it the same as being "filled" with the Spirit.

- Stated: 1 Corinthians 12:13

- Significance:
  - All of His is _____ (1 Cor. 1:30–31; John 15:20).
  - He cares for us (2 Cor. 4:7–12).
  - We are _____ with other believers (Eph. 3:1–6; 1 Cor. 8).

Sealing

- Defined:

  _____

  _____

  _____

- Stated: Ephesians 1:13–14; 4:30

- Significance:

  - _____

  - _____ (Gal. 5:22–23)

  - _____ (Gal. 2:20; 4:7)

Application Activities

1. Read Acts 4–5, and record each truth about the Holy Spirit that you find in these chapters.

2. Read Acts 15:1–35, which describes the Jerusalem Council. In one page or less, describe the issue discussed by the council and how they addressed it. In what way do you think the Holy Spirit worked through this process? Note that Paul wrote the Epistle to the Galatians around the time of this discussion.

3. Record your salvation experience, noting the people and circumstances God used to draw you to Himself. In what specific ways do you believe that His Spirit convicted and changed you?

4. List at least six passages that address the Holy Spirit's work in salvation, and summarize the core messages of each.

5. In three paragraphs or less, explain why simple *conviction* of sin does not mean salvation. What must come afterward? How else does the Spirit work in us to lead us to Christ?

CHAPTER 34

The Holy Spirit's Work in Sanctification

"I cannot live the Christian life by making up my mind I am going to live that life. I cannot live the Christian life by any fleshly activity or mental cleverness. I must have, and be filled with, this Holy Spirit. Our churches can do nothing which is really effective for the Kingdom of God without the Spirit."

—G. Campbell Morgan, "The Mediating Ministry of the Holy Spirit,"
The Best of G. Campbell Morgan

All true Christians recognize the work of God in salvation. As sinful as we are, we cannot possibly earn our way into God's family. God must accomplish this by His grace. The Spirit of God must convict, regenerate, baptize, indwell, and seal us. We know that we cannot do any of this for ourselves.

But many Christians forget that they still need the Spirit *after* salvation. We cannot do good things or become more holy except through Him. He alone makes us better vessels for God. He alone is our strength to serve others. He alone pulls us above the sinful desires of our flesh, pointing our attention instead to God Himself.

To make this point clear, the Spirit inspired an entire book—the Epistle to the Galatians—to convince us that we need God's grace always. We accepted salvation and the Spirit by faith (Gal. 3:13–14), and we must continue to live by faith. We must walk in step with the Spirit (Gal. 5:16–26), because He alone will create in us the love and goodness of God.

As we walk with Him, we will not submit to sin—nor will we believe that we can become more holy by doing good things or by following the Law. As

Paul wrote in Galatians 3:19–29, God gave us the Law to teach us what sin is. It does not by itself show us the life we should live in the Spirit. Obedience *reveals* love (John 14:15), but it does not *create* love.

We therefore depend on God's goodness and grace for both salvation and sanctification. We cannot *be* or *do* better through sheer willpower, through busyness, or through any act of our own. We cannot earn God's love now— any more than we could before we accepted Christ.

We simply commune with God in prayer and the Word, ask Him to make us better reflections of Him, and then trust the Spirit to work through us as we show His love to others.

Thankfully, there will never come a day when we cannot meet with God. We can always seek and find Him, even if we do not always understand His work. The skies will grow dark, the people we love will pull away, and our own strength will fail—but the Spirit dwells inside of us, and we can trust Him to preserve and protect us until we see God face-to-face.

Student Work

Other Ministries of the Holy Spirit

He Gives Gifts

✎ A *spiritual gift* is a God-given ability for service. Read 1 Corinthians 12:8–11 and answer the following:

- Whose work or power did these gifts represent (v. 11)?

  _____

- How were recipients of these gifts chosen (v. 11)?

  _____

  _____

  _____

✎ List all of the gifts mentioned in the following passages. Though some gifts are mentioned in more than one passage, you can list each gift only once.

- Romans 12:6–8

  _____

  _____

  _____

- 1 Corinthians 12:8–10

  _____

  _____

  _____

  _____

- 1 Corinthians 12:28–30

  _____

  _____

The Holy Spirit will give these abilities as He desires, and it is our responsibility to discover and develop them as we serve others.

Are all of these gifts present today in the same form? Some, such as predictive prophecy and the gift of tongues, are not. These signs clearly marked the approval of God over the early church, but as 1 Corinthians 13:8 implies, tongues and prophecies would not last.

Christ did not intend for people to accept Him through miraculous signs and wonders. After all, these deeds did not create lasting followers during His earthly ministry. He draws people to Himself through the invisible work of the Spirit (John 16:8), through the teaching of His Word (Rom. 10:14), and through the love of His people (John 13:35).

He Fills

In the Old Testament, we read of people "filled" with the Spirit who do extraordinary things. And in the New Testament, we read that all believers have the Spirit (Rom. 8:9), but some—like Stephen and the first deacons—are especially filled with Him. What then does this *filling* mean?

✎ Read Ephesians 5:18–21. Paul contrasts being "filled with the Spirit" with what state of mind (v. 18)? _____

We should not let ourselves be controlled by substances like alcohol—instead, we should submit ourselves to the control of the Spirit. As Paul wrote in Galatians 5, we must walk in step with the Spirit, acknowledging His control and reflecting His character.

Therefore, to be filled with the Spirit is to reflect Him by who we are, by the way we think, and by what we do. He fills Christians who embody His love and truth.

Note that Paul phrased verse 18 in the form of an imperative—"be filled with the Spirit." Though the Spirit Himself accomplishes this work, it will not occur if we do not submit to Him. We can refuse this filling by committing sins that grieve Him—or by trusting in our own strength to do right.

✎ In the following blanks, summarize the actions associated with being filled with the Spirit. Note that verse 19 lists two actions.

- Verse 19

  _____

  _____

  _____

- Verse 20

  _____

  _____

- Verse 21

  _____

  _____

When the Spirit fills us, we will overflow with praise to God. We will worship God with our hearts and with other people. And as we learn to reverence God, we will respect His children and submit ourselves to each other.

✎ List the fruit of the Spirit, as given in Galatians 5:22–23.

_____

_____

_____

He Helps Us Pray

✎ Read Romans 8:26–28. According to verse 26, what *don't* we know?

_____

_____

✎ What then does the Spirit do (v. 26)?

_____

_____

_____

Since the Spirit, as God, knows the mind of the Father, He presents our needs in perfect parallel with the will of God (v. 27).

✎ Write Romans 8:28 below:

_____

_____

_____

_____

We believers may not know exactly what to pray, but we *do* know that God works everything for our good. It's comforting to know that the God who dwells in us is the God who intercedes for us—and is the God who bends the universe toward our good.

Does that mean we shouldn't pray? By no means. We pray to commune with the God we love and need. Romans 8 merely assures us that we don't need to worry about always praying for the right things in the right way. The Spirit takes care of that for us, and God works toward our good regardless. And as we meditate on Him over time, our prayers will better reflect His purpose and desire.

He Gives Assurance

✎ Write Romans 8:16 below:

_____

_____

_____

_____

The Holy Spirit Himself testifies to our own spirit that we are God's children (cf. 1 John 3:24; 4:13). Therefore, if you doubt your salvation, one of the following may be true:

- **You have not accepted Christ**, and you are therefore not one of God's children.
- **You are not listening to the Spirit**, who reveals His presence and truth through the Word and through prayer.

Many Christians have at some point questioned their salvation. They may wonder if they prayed the right kind of prayer or did the right things.

But remember: God does not save anyone based on what he or she does. We do not earn salvation by praying the right words the right way at the right time. Rather, God saves those people who trust Him for salvation. At the moment of salvation, we simply believe in the *Lord Jesus Christ* (Acts 16:29–31):

- **Jesus**—because He is the real, historical figure who died and rose from the dead
- **Christ**—because He is the Anointed One sent to save us from sin
- **Lord**—because He is God our Ruler, deserving of all our worship and obedience, the One with the standing to forgive us if we ask

People need not have a perfect understanding of salvation when they accept Christ. The doctrines here are deep and incomprehensible, and each day we can learn new ways to acknowledge Jesus as our Messiah and God. But as we study God's Word and grow in His knowledge, His Spirit will assure us of God's presence in our hearts. We will learn to trust that God saves those who accept His Son.

. . . .

Notes from the Teacher's Lesson

The Sanctification of the Spirit

- _____ (1 Cor. 6:9–11; Rom. 6:17–18)
- _____ (1 Cor. 2:1–5)

- _____ (Eph. 3:14–19; Ps. 18:31–32)
- _____ (Eph. 3:4–6; 4:1–6)

Walking with the Spirit *(Gal. 5:17)*

- _____ His presence (Rom. 8:9).
- _____ on His truth through the Word (Rom. 12:2).
- _____ to Him (John 16:12–15; 1 Thess. 5:19).
- _____ the flesh (Rom. 13:14).

Application Activities

1. Read Acts 6 and 8, and record every way you can find that the Spirit worked in these chapters. Write a brief summary of each work, along with the reference.

2. Record a providence from any category in which the Holy Spirit clearly guided believers through a situation.

3. List three examples of situations in which it is especially helpful that the Holy Spirit can intercede for us. At what times do we simply not know how to pray?

4. Read 1 Corinthians 14, and create an outline of requirements governing the use of tongues. Preface this outline with a paragraph describing the gift of tongues, as presented in Scripture.

5. If you have already completed Activity 4, research the doctrines of at least two denominations that currently practice the gift of tongues. Describe their doctrine in two pages or less.

- According to their teaching, what is the purpose of tongues, and how do they appear in worship or sermons?
- Does this kind of practice match with the gifts described in Scripture?
- Cite your sources where appropriate.

CHAPTER 35

The First-Claim Principle

"What comes into our minds when we think about God is the most important thing about us."

—A. W. Tozer, *The Knowledge of the Holy*

Throughout this study, you've read countless statements of God's power, goodness, and holiness. He is omnipotent, He is loving, He is perfect, and He is exalted. It's comforting to know that He works in every circumstance ultimately to bring good to us and glory to Himself. You might admit this truth, but it's time to build your life on it.

As we've seen over and over again, God's wisdom does not always match our own. He calls leaders servants, not authoritarians. He makes no distinctions between male and female, Jew or Gentile, bond or free—He calls us all to speak truth in love, orderliness, and understanding, despite our differences. He calls us to be holy, yet we cannot answer this call in our own strength.

Take time at the end of this study to examine your thoughts and actions in light of what you've learned. Do you pursue the knowledge of God? Do you compare your character with His? Do you discipline your thoughts to mirror His? Do you serve others humbly as Christ did?

As you complete this study, commit yourself to knowing God, and ask Him to reveal Himself *to* and *through* you. Abide in His truth and love, and you will shine His light to the world.

Student Work

✎ Write Colossians 1:18 below:

_____

_____

_____

_____

_____

✎ For each area of life listed, provide at least two relevant passages of
Scripture that teach us how to honor and follow Christ first. Then record
any key truths or principles you find in those passages.

Everyday Activities

• Scripture: _____

• Principles:

_____

_____

_____

College or Higher Education

• Scripture: _____

• Principles:

_____

_____

_____

Career

• Scripture: _____

• Principles:

_____

_____

_____

Finances

- Scripture: _____

- Principles:

  _____

  _____

  _____

Relationships and Marriage

- Scripture: _____

- Principles:

  _____

  _____

  _____

Raising Children

- Scripture: _____

- Principles:

  _____

  _____

  _____

Community Involvement

- Scripture: _____

- Principles:

  _____

  _____

  _____

Ministry Within the Church

- Scripture:_____

- Principles:

  _____

  _____

  _____

Music, Literature, and the Arts

- Scripture: _____

- Principles:

  _____

  _____

  _____

Ongoing Learning and Discovery

- Scripture: _____

- Principles:

  _____

  _____

  _____

Personal Health

- Scripture: _____

- Principles:

  _____

  _____

  _____

Notes from the Teacher's Lesson

The First-Claim Principle *(Matt. 6:33; Luke 9:57–62)*

The Basis of the Principle

- Who Christ is:

  ○ He is _____ (Rom. 14:7–11)

  ○ He is _____
    (Eph. 1:22–23; Col. 1:15–20)

- What Christ has done for us (Phil. 2:5–11; 1 Cor. 6:19–20)

The Application of the Principle

Under each category, write examples of what we should submit to Christ.

- Our _____ (Eph. 5:15–17)

  _____

  _____

  _____

  _____

  _____

- Our _____ (Matt. 6:33)

  _____

  _____

  _____

  _____

  _____

- Our _____ (Col. 3:2)

  _____

  _____

  _____

  _____

  _____

- Our _____ (Prov. 3:9; 2 Cor. 8:1–5)

  _____

  _____

  _____

  _____

  _____

- Our _____ (2 Cor. 10:5; Rom. 12:1–2)

  _____

  _____

  _____

  _____

  _____

Application Activities

1. Interview a Christian whose testimony and ministry you admire. Ask this person how God directed him or her to choose a career or life's work. Record and summarize the person's answers in a page or less.

2. Find and read a book on time management—or at least ten articles from reputable sources. Summarize what you learn in a one page paper, and explain—preferably with a table—how you intend to budget your time after the end of this academic term. Note: your teacher might help you identify reputable sources.

3. For each of the following occupations, briefly explain how Christians can pursue it as a full-time ministry, regardless of whether they are paid by a church or Christian organization.

   - Doctor / Medical Occupations
   - Lawyer
   - Engineer
   - Architect
   - Software Engineer / Developer
   - Writer / Editor
   - Accountant
   - Insurance agent
   - Mathematician
   - Chemist
   - Salesperson
   - Mechanic
   - And two other occupations of your choice